CBSE
Chapterwise
SOLVED PAPERS
2022-2010

Physical
Education
Class **XII**

CBSE
Chapterwise
SOLVED PAPERS
2022-2010

Physical
Education
Class **XII**

Authors
Rakesh Kumar Roshan
Reena kar

arihant
ARIHANT PRAKASHAN (School Division Series)

☸ ADMINISTRATIVE & PRODUCTION OFFICES

Regd. Office

'Ramchhaya' 4577/15, Agarwal Road, Darya Ganj, New Delhi -110002
Tele: 011- 47630600, 43518550

Head Office

Kalindi, TP Nagar, Meerut (UP) - 250002, Tel: 0121-7156203, 7156204

☸ SALES & SUPPORT OFFICES

Agra, Ahmedabad, Bengaluru, Bareilly, Chennai, Delhi, Guwahati, Hyderabad, Jaipur, Jhansi, Kolkata, Lucknow, Nagpur & Pune.

PO No : TXT-XX-XXXXXXX-X-XX

Published By Arihant Publications (India) Ltd.

For further information about the books published by Arihant, log on to www.arihantbooks.com or e-mail at info@arihantbooks.com

Follow us on

☸ ISBN

9 789326 198684

PREFACE

The school examinations play the most important role in the life of any student. Also in today's scenario, the importance of school examination is maximum as ever, government has fixed the weightage of these examinations in the process of admission to any higher level education programme.

Now, the question rises what should be the way of study to get higher percentage of marks. The answer is simple that we should plan our way of studies in such a way that along with the school studies we should also keep an eye on what type of questions are being asked in the real examinations and what can be better than that if we practice the real examination questions in a chapterwise manner which are further divided into topics, it is the same way in which we study in our classroom.

To serve this purpose, here we are presenting CBSE Chapterwise Solved Papers Physical Education containing Previous Years' Questions-Answers asked in CBSE Class 12th Examination. At the end of the book **3 Sample Question Papers** have been given. The questions in each topic have been arranged as per their marks and in the descending chronological order i.e., 1 Mark Questions, 2 Marks, 3 Marks Questions and 5 Marks Questions. The next important feature of the book is, the answers to all the questions have been given according to CBSE Marking Scheme. This book for sure will prove to be the most important tool in getting a high end success in CBSE Class 12th Examination.

We have put my best efforts in preparing this book, but if any error or what so ever has been skipped out, then that is purely incidental, apology for the same, please write to us so that it can be corrected in the further edition of the book. Apart from all those who helped in the compilation of this book a special note of thanks to Shivam Gupta.

At the end, we wish Best of Luck to our readers !

Rakesh Kumar Roshan
Reena Kar

CONTENTS

1. Management of Sporting Events 1-13
2. Children and Women in Sports 14-21
3. Yoga and Lifestyle 22-43
4. Physical Education & Sports for CWSN 44-51
5. Sports and Nutrition 52-59
6. Test and Measurement in Sports 60-69
7. Physiology and Injuries in Sports 70-81
8. Biomechanics and Sports 82-89
9. Psychology and Sports 90-95
10. Training in Sports 96-106

• **Sample Question Papers** (1-3) **109-133**

LATEST SYLLABUS

Max. Marks 70

UNIT I Management of Sporting Events

- Functions of Sports Events Management (Planning, Organising, Staffing, Directing & Controlling)
- Various Committees & their Responsibilities (pre; during & post)
- Fixtures and its Procedures – Knock-Out (Bye & Seeding) & League (Staircase & Cyclic)

UNIT II Children & Women in Sports

- Common Postural Deformities - Knock Knee; Bow Legs; Flat Foot; Round Shoulders; Lordosis, Kyphosis, and Scoliosis and their corrective measures
- Special consideration (Menarche & Menstrual Dysfunction)
- Female Athletes Triad (Osteoporosis, Amenorrhea, Eating Disorders)

UNIT III Yoga as Preventive Measure for Lifestyle Disease

- Obesity: Procedure, Benefits & Contraindications for Tadasana, Katichakrasana, Pavanmuktasana, Matsayasana, Halasana, Pachimottansana, Ardha – Matsyendrasana, Dhanurasana, Ushtrasana, Suryabedhan pranayama.
- Diabetes: Procedure, Benefits & Contraindications for Katichakrasana, Pavanmuktasana, Bhujangasana, Shalabhasana, Dhanurasana, Supta-vajarasana, Paschimottanasana, Ardha-Mastendrasana, Mandukasana, Gomukasana, Yogmudra, Ushtrasana, Kapalabhati.
- Asthma: Procedure, Benefits & Contraindications for Tadasana, Urdhwahastottansana, UttanMandukasana, Bhujangasana, Dhanurasana, Ushtrasana, Vakrasana, Kapalbhati, Gomukhasana, Matsyaasana, Anuloma-Viloma.
- Hypertension: Procedure, Benefits & Contraindications for Tadasana, Katichakransan, Uttanpadasana, Ardha Halasana, Sarala Matyasana, Gomukhasana, UttanMandukasana, Vakrasana, Bhujangasana, Makarasana, Shavasana, Nadi-shodhanapranayam, Sitlipranayam.

UNIT IV Physical Education & Sports for CWSN (Children with Special Needs-Divyang)

- Organizations promoting Disability Sports (Special Olympics; Paralympics; Deaflympics)
- Advantages of Physical Activities for children with special needs.
- Strategies to make Physical Activities assessable for children with special needs.

UNIT V Sports & Nutrition

- Concept of balance diet and nutrition
- Macro and Micro Nutrients: Food sources & functions
- Nutritive & Non-Nutritive Components of Diet

UNIT VI Test & Measurement in Sports

- Fitness Test – SAI Khelo India Fitness Test in school:
  - Age group 5-8 yrs/ class 1-3: BMI, Flamingo Balance Test, Plate Tapping Test
  - Age group 9-18yrs/ class 4-12: BMI, 50mt Speed test, 600mt Run/Walk, Sit & Reach flexibility test, Strength Test (Abdominal Partial Curl Up, Push-Ups for boys, Modified Push-Ups for girls).
- Computing Basal Metabolic Rate (BMR)
- Rikli & Jones - Senior Citizen Fitness Test
  - i. Chair Stand Test for lower body strength
  - ii. Arm Curl Test for upper body strength
  - iii. Chair Sit & Reach Test for lower body flexibility
  - iv. Back Scratch Test for upper body flexibility
  - v. Eight Foot Up & Go Test for agility
  - vi. Six Minute Walk Test for Aerobic Endurance

UNIT VII Physiology & Injuries in Sports

- Physiological factors determining components of physical fitness
- Effect of exercise on Muscular System
- Effect of exercise on Cardio-Respiratory System
- Sports injuries: Classification (Soft Tissue Injuries -Abrasion, Contusion, Laceration, Incision, Sprain & Strain; Bone & Joint Injuries - Dislocation, Fractures - Green Stick, Comminuted, Transverse Oblique & Impacted)

UNIT VIII Biomechanics & Sports

- Newton's Law of Motion & its application in sports
- Equilibrium – Dynamic & Static and Centre of Gravity and its application in sports
- Friction & Sports
- Projectile in Sports

UNIT IX Psychology & Sports

- Personality; its definition & types (Jung Classification & Big Five Theory)
- Meaning, Concept & Types of Aggressions in Sports
- Psychological Attributes in Sports – Self Esteem, Mental Imagery, Self Talk, Goal Setting

UNIT X Training in Sports

- Concept of Talent Identification and Talent Development in Sports
- Introduction to Sports Training Cycle – Micro, Meso, Macro Cycle.
- Types & Method to Develop – Strength, Endurance and Speed
- Types & Method to Develop – Flexibility and Coordinative Ability

PRACTICAL

Max. Marks 30

01.	Physical Fitness Test: SAI Khelo India test, Brockport Physical Fitness Test (BPFT) *	6 Marks
02.	Proficiency in Games & Sports (Skill of any one IOA recognised Sport/Game of choice) **	7 Marks
03.	Yogic Practices	7 Marks
04.	Record File***	5 Marks
05.	Viva Voce (Health/Games & Sports/Yoga)	5 Marks

* Test for CWSN (any 4 items out of 27items. One item from each component: Aerobic Function, Body Composition, Muscular Strength & Endurance, Range of Motion or Flexibility)

**CWSN (Children With Special Needs – Divyang): Bocce/Boccia , Sitting Volleyball, Wheel Chair Basketball, Unified Badminton, Unified Basketball, Unified Football, Blind Cricket, Goalball, Floorball, Wheel Chair Races and Throws, or any other Sport/Game of choice.

**Children With Special Needs can also opt any one Sport/Game from the list as alternative to Yogic Practices. However, the Sport/Game must be different from Test- 'Proficiency in Games & Sports'.

***Record File shall include:
- Practical-1: Fitness tests administration.
- Practical-2: Procedure for Asanas, Benefits & Contraindication for any two Asanas for each lifestyle disease.
- Practical-3: Any one IOA recognised Sport/Game of choice. Labelled diagram of Field & Equipment. Also mention its Rules, Terminologies & Skills.

CHAPTER 01

Management of Sporting Events

Sports events create opportunities for people to connect with an area, spend time together, celebrate and experience the diversity of cultures, foster creativity and innovation. Sports events are important for the all round development of children and youths.

Sports and physical education are an integral part of the learning process. Physical education plays an important role in the overall development of an individual. The primary goal of physical education in school is to teach essential skills to students and support their health.

Functions of Sports Events Management

Sports event whose concept came in 1950's in India when the Asian Game was hosted in New Delhi from where the establishment of sporting event management started. Sports event management helps in organise the sports events in short interval of time.

It gives an opportunity to work on project from their conceptualisation to their eventual execution. The management functions includes planning, organising, placing, directing and controlling.

Important functions of sports events management are given below

Planning

Planning means to organise the activities in order to reach a particular goal. It is like deciding in advance, what is to be done, how it is to be done and by whom it is to be done.

In other words, planning is a process of setting goals, outlining tasks, developing strategies and schedules to accomplish desired goals.

Planning is needed for management of tournaments like formation of different committees, organisation of intramural and extramural activities, arrangement of various types of fixtures in sports, mass participation, programmes for fitness, etc.

Organising

It includes distributing resources and organising personnel in order to achieve the goals established in the sports events planning functions. It includes organising and division of work, departmentalisation, assignment of duties and establishing reporting relationship.

Staffing

Staffing refers to identifying key staff positions and to ensuring that the proper talent is serving that specific job duty in order to achieve the aims and objectives of an organisation. Sports events typically have a team based work environment and a Project type of organisation structure and that reponsibility are assigned to relevant staff members in the team for the event.

Directing

Directing personnel is a leadership quality and includes letting staff know what needs to be done and also by when. It includes supervision of personnel while simultaneously motivating them. It helps to initiate action by people in the organisation towards attainment of desired objectives.

Controlling

It refers to all the processes that leaders create to monitor success. It involves establishing performance standards, measuring actual performance, comparing its irregularities, analysing deviations and taking correct measures.

Various Committees and their Responsibilities

Examples of some committees (pre, during and post) formed for conducting a sports event or a tournament are given below

- (*i*) **Committee for Publicity** Its main duty is to advertise the sports events.
- (*ii*) **Transport Committee** Its main responsibility is to make necessary arrangements for transportation of officials, competitors and guests.
- (*iii*) **Grounds and Equipment Committee** This committee is responsible for proper upkeep of the venues and making the necessary equipment available for conducting the events.
- (*iv*) **Refreshments and Entertainment Committee** This committee takes the charge of supplying refreshments and drinks to the guests, officials, competitors, etc.
- (*v*) **Reception Committee** The members of this committee are responsible to welcome the Chief Guest and the spectators at the opening and closing ceremonies.
- (*vi*) **Committee on Entries and Programmes** This committee sends entry forms to the participating institutions well in time. It also arranges seats for guests and spectators. It sometimes also prepares fixtures of teams participating in the competition.

- (*vii*) **Committee for Officials** This committee selects various officials such as referees, judges, umpires, etc.
- (*viii*) **Announcement Committee** This committee is responsible for making all the announcements during the period of sports events.
- (*ix*) **First Aid Committee** This committee provides first aid to the victims or affected sportsman/athlete.
- (*x*) **Protest Committee** It decides on any protest made against a judgement in any part of a tournament.
- (*xi*) **Finance Committee** It makes the budget and controls the expenses of a tournament.

For successful organisation of a sports meet, committees may be formed under three heads. These are pre-meet committees such as publicity, ground and equipment, reception committee; during meet committees such as refreshment, transport committee; and post-meet committees such as award committee.

Pre, During and Post-meet Responsibilities of Committees

The entire arrangement and planning for a sports event is organised in three phases; pre, during and post-meet work. These three phases are separate phases yet their functions can be overlapping.

They are discussed below

Pre-meet Responsibilities of Committees

Before an organisation starts a tournament, there are various preparations that are required for the event. These are known as the pre-meet responsibilities that an organisation needs to tackle before starting of the sports event.

Pre-meet responsibilities are as follows

- To prepare the budget for organising the sports event.
- To organise meeting of important officials to fix the venue, date and timings of the sports event.

- To prepare a list of events, ceremonies and entertainment programmes that will be covered during the event.
- To appoint different officials that are going to judge the sports events as well as invite a chief guest.
- To form various committees and list their tasks accordingly.
- To publicise about the sports event in the newspapers, send invitations to other institutions, distribute pamphlets, posters, etc.
- To make necessary arrangements for preparation of ground, equipment, lodging, prizes, certificates, etc.

Responsibilities of During-meet Committees

There are a lot of work that needs to be undertaken when the sports event is taking place. These are called as during-meet responsibilities.

They are as follows

- To check that all the equipment, ground, stadiums and the places where sports events are held, are in proper condition.
- To check that the lodging facilities of outstation candidates and refreshments of all the participants are adequate.
- To keep a record of all the events, their winners and check that the events are taking place as per schedule.
- To check the work of all other committees simultaneously.
- To make important announcements about the progress of the event.
- To provide first-aid and medical aid wherever needed during the entire event.

Responsibilities of Post-meet Committees

The major portion of the work that is done after the event is over or towards the end of the event are known as post-meet responsibilities. They are as follows

- To check that the outstanding bills are paid.
- To prepare a list of income and expenses.

- To return all the borrowed equipments in proper condition.
- To acknowledge the services of volunteers, officials, staff, workers who were associated during the event in the closing ceremony.
- To release press and media news related to the event.
- To preserve the records of the sports events, timings etc.
- To see that the prizes, trophies, medals, certificates are handed over to the winners in proper way.
- To provide security refunds wherever applicable.
- To present mementos to the chief guests or guest of honour, etc.

Fixture and its Procedures

Any tournament, whether it is knock-out or league, is arranged according to a set procedure which is known as fixture. For a knock-out tournament, the procedure to draw fixtures is through bye and seeding.

For a league tournaments, the procedure to draw fixtures is through staircase or cyclic method.

Fixture is the process of arranging the teams in systematic order in various groups for competition in a physical activity. In other words, it is the arrangement of competition between various teams in matches in which they play in a systematic order as per the fixture schedule. The success of a tournament depends upon planning of a suitable fixture schedule. Tournaments are played in various forms of fixtures.

Fixtures in Knock-out Tournament

In a knock-out tournament, the fixtures are drawn by any of the following methods.

1. Seeding Method

Seeding is a procedure by which good teams are placed in fixtures in such a way that stronger teams do not meet each other at the very start of a tournament. It is done to overcome the drawbacks of a single knock-out tournament.

Seeding can be done only if the standards of the teams are known before the start of the tournament. The draw may result between the strong competitors at early level competition, so they are 'seeded' to prevent this. Thus, the top competitors will not meet until the quarter final, semi final or final round. Seeding is used to ensure that players or teams of recognised outstanding ability do not confront each other in the early rounds. It represents the tournament committee's subjective rating of the various players, and chances of winning the tournament.

Special Seeding

It is a method of seeding in which certain players or teams directly participate in the quarter final or semi-final matches thus avoiding their participation in the initial rounds.

2. Bye Method

Bye means the avoiding of playing a match in the first round of the tournament. It is a privilege given to a team which is decided generally by seeding it or by draw of lots. Some teams may get bye in first round, by which they get promoted to a higher round competition.

This may be given as a reward for their previous achievements. Byes can be applied equally to single person competitions and team sports as well as to single game eliminations and best of series elimination. Byes are given in Ist round only.

The number of byes that should be given in a tournament is decided by finding the difference between the number of teams and the next power of two.

Example : $(N-1)$ if 20 teams are participating, then 19 matches $(20-1)=19$ will be played.

Method of Drawing Fixtures in Knock-out Tournament

In order to draw fixtures in a knock-out tournament, it is essential to calculate

1. **Total Number of Matches** It means the total number of matches that will be played during the entire tournament. The number of matches to be played is calculated by subtracting 1 from total number of teams $(N-1)$.

   Suppose total teams are 11. So the matches to be played during the tournament are 10 $(11-1)$.

2. **Number of Rounds** It means the total number of rounds that should be played during the tournament. Rounds will include the initial rounds, quarter finals, semi finals and finals. If the number of teams is a power of 2, then number of rounds will exactly be multiple of 2 upto that number.

   Example :

   16 teams, rounds = $\underset{\textcircled{1}\ \textcircled{2}\ \textcircled{3}\ \textcircled{4}}{2 \times 2 \times 2 \times 2 = 4 \text{ rounds}}$

   If number of teams is not a power of 2, then number of rounds will be equal to the multiple of next power of two.

   Example :

   21 teams, round $\underset{2 \times 2 \times 2 \times 2 \times 2 = 5 \text{ rounds}}{\overset{\textcircled{1}\ \textcircled{2}\ \textcircled{3}\ \textcircled{4}\ \textcircled{5}}{}}$

   The next power of 2 after 21 is 32 which is 2^5.

3. **Number of Teams in Each Half** All the teams are divided into two halves for the sake of convenience. If the number of teams is even, then the number of teams in upper and lower half will be equal. For instance, if the total number of teams are 20, then apply the formula $\dfrac{N}{2}$.

   Number of teams in upper half $=\dfrac{N}{2}=\dfrac{20}{2}=10$

   Number of teams in lower half $=\dfrac{N}{2}=\dfrac{20}{2}=10$

   If the number of teams is odd, then apply $\dfrac{N+1}{2}$ for upper half and $\dfrac{N-1}{2}$ for lower half.

   Example : Total teams $= 15$

   Number of teams in upper half

   $$\dfrac{N+1}{2} = \dfrac{15+1}{2} = 8$$

   Number of teams in lower half

   $$\dfrac{N-1}{2} = \dfrac{15-1}{2} = 7$$

4. **Number of Byes** Teams getting the byes do not play in the initial round. The number of teams which are given byes can be found by subtracting the number of teams from the next higher power of 2.

   Example 1 : Total number of teams = 19
   Next higher power of two = 32
   (Power of two – 2^1, $2^2 = 4$, $2^3 = 8$, $2^4 = 16$, $2^5 = 32$ and so on)
   therefore number of byes will be $32 - 19 = 13$

   Example 2 : Total number of teams = 12
   Next higher power of two = 16
   Therefore number of byes $16 - 12 = 4$

   Hence, 13 teams in example 1 and 4 teams in example 2 will not play a match in the 1st round.

5. **Number of Byes in Upper and Lower Half**
   For calculating how many teams in upper and lower half will get byes, the method is as follows

   Number of byes in upper half $= \dfrac{Nb - 1}{2}$

   Number of byes in lower half $= \dfrac{Nb + 1}{2}$

   Where Nb = total number of byes = 13

   Number of byes in upper half $= \dfrac{13 - 1}{2} = 6$

   Number of byes in lower half $= \dfrac{13 + 1}{2} = 7$

6. **Method of Fixing Byes** The teams are placed in upper and lower half according to a draw of lots or by using other methods. *Then the following procedure is adopted for fixing the byes*
   The last team of lower half gets the first bye.
   The first team of upper half gets the second bye.
   The first team of lower half gets the third bye.
   The last team of upper half gets the fourth bye.
   The second last team of lower half gets the fifth bye.
   Like this the order continues.

Example : A fixture of 19 teams on knock-out basis.

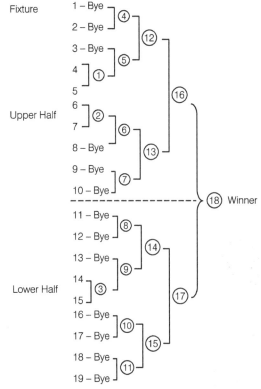

Total matches $N - 1 = 19 - 1 = 18$

Number of teams in upper half
$$= \frac{N + 1}{2} = \frac{19 + 1}{2} = \frac{20}{2} = 10 \text{ teams}$$

Number of teams in lower half
$$= \frac{N - 1}{2} = \frac{19 - 1}{2} = \frac{18}{2} = 9 \text{ teams}$$

Total number of byes
$$= \text{Next power of two – Total}$$
number of teams $= 32 - 19 = 13$ byes

Number of byes in upper half
$$= \frac{\text{Total number of byes} - 1}{2}$$

i.e. $\left(\dfrac{Nb - 1}{2}\right) = \dfrac{13 - 1}{2} = \dfrac{12}{2} = 6$ byes

Number of byes in lower half

$$= \frac{\text{Total number of byes} + 1}{2}$$

i.e. $\left(\dfrac{Nb+1}{2}\right) = \dfrac{13+1}{2} = \dfrac{14}{2} = 7$ byes

7. **Method of Seeding** It is done to prevent the strong teams from competing with each other in the initial round. Therefore the strong teams are placed in the position where they will get a bye i.e. placing the strong teams on the last position of lower half or first position of upper half.

Example 1 : Total number of teams = 6

Next higher power of two = 8

Number of byes = 8 − 6 = 2

Seeding is done for the last team of lower half and first team of upper half.

Number of matches 6 − 1 = 5

Example 2 : A fixture of 12 teams where 4 teams getting special seeding.

Total number of teams = 12

Number of teams in upper half $= \dfrac{N}{2} = \dfrac{12}{2} = 6$

Number of teams in lower half $= \dfrac{N}{2} = 6$

Teams setting special seeding = 4

Number of matches = 12 − 1 = 11

Fixture

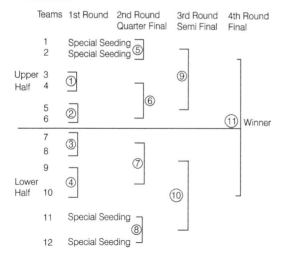

Remarks

- Team numbers 1, 2, 11 and 12 do not play in the first round as they get special seeding.
- Winner of each bracket enters the next round while losers are eliminated. For instance, Team 3 and 4 play match number 1. If 3 wins, then 4 is eliminated from the tournament.

Fixtures in League Tournaments

The three methods used for drawing up fixtures in league tournaments are

1. Staircase method
2. Cyclic method

1. Staircase Method

In this method, the fixtures are made similar to a staircase. They are arranged in sequential form, there is no bye and no problem of odd or even. Therefore it is easiest to arrange. An example will illustrate this method.

Example : Draw up a fixture of 9 teams on Round Robin basis using staircase method.

The number of teams = 9

Thus, number of matches

$$= \frac{N(N-1)}{2} = \frac{9\,(9-1)}{2}$$

$$= \frac{9 \times 8}{2} = 36 \text{ matches}$$

The fixture is given below

1-2							
1-3	2-3						
1-4	2-4	3-4					
1-5	2-5	3-5	4-5				
1-6	2-6	3-6	4-6	5-6			
1-7	2-7	3-7	4-7	5-7	6-7		
1-8	2-8	3-8	4-8	5-8	6-8	7-8	
1-9	2-9	3-9	4-9	5-9	6-9	7-9	8-9

2. Cyclic Method

In this method, if the number of teams is even (i.e. 4, 6, 8, ...), team 1 is fixed on the top right side and the other teams move in clockwise direction down one side of a rectangle and up on the other side. In such a case, the number of rounds will be N-1 if there are N teams participating. However, if the number of teams is odd (i.e. 3, 5, 7, ...), a 'bye' is fixed at the top and all teams follow it in sequence. In such a case, the number of rounds will be N.

Example 1 Fixture of 6 teams on cyclic method.

Total number of teams = 6

$$\text{Total number of matches } = \frac{N(N-1)}{2}$$

$$= \frac{6(6-1)}{2} = 15$$

Total number of rounds $= N - 1 = 5$

Round	1st R	2nd R	3rd R	4th R	5th R
	6 ↔ ①	5 ↔ ①	4 ↔ ①	3 ↔ ①	2 ↔ ①
	5 ↔ 2	4 ↔ 6	3 ↔ 5	2 ↔ 4	6 ↔ 3
	4 ↔ 3	3 ↔ 2	2 ↔ 6	6 ↔ 5	5 ↔ 4

Example 2 Fixture of 5 teams on cyclic method.

Total number of teams = 5

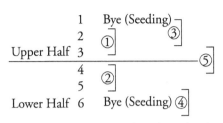

$$\text{Total number of matches} = \frac{N(N-1)}{2} = \frac{5(5-1)}{2} = 10$$

Total number of rounds = 5

Round	1st R	2nd R	3rd R	4th R	5th R
	5 ↔ Bye	4 ↔ Bye	3 ↔ Bye	2 ↔ Bye	1 ↔ Bye
	4 ↔ 1	3 ↔ 5	2 ↔ 4	1 ↔ 3	5 ↔ 2
	3 ↔ 2	2 ↔ 1	1 ↔ 5	5 ↔ 4	4 ↔ 3

Deciding the Winner

The method to decide the winner in league tournaments is by calculating the percentage of matches won.

$$\text{Percentage} = \frac{\text{Matches won}}{\text{Matches played}} \times 100$$

Normally, there are two points for every match won and zero for every match lost. But in case of a draw, each team is given one point. However there can be several other ways of calculating the winner.

Previous Years'

Examination & Other Important Questions

☑ 1 Mark Questions (MCQ)

1. Which of the following is a function of sports event management?
(a) Organising
(b) Directing
(c) Staffing
(b) All of the above

Ans. *(d)* All of the above

2. The Reception Committee for a tournament is responsible for ....
(a) welcoming the participants
(b) arranging accommodation and meals for the participants
(c) proper upkeep of the venues
(d) welcoming the Chief Guest and spectators at the opening and closing ceremonies

Ans. *(d)* welcoming the Chief Guest and spectators at the opening and closing ceremonies

3. The Boarding and Lodging Committee for a tournament arranges ....
(a) the making of the budget for boarding and lodging
(b) meals, refreshment and stay of the Chief Guest
(c) accommodation and meals for the participants
(d) refreshments for the participants and officials

Ans. *(c)* accommodation and meals for the participants

4. Which of the following procedures is not used for drawing up fixtures for a knockout tournament?
(a) Bye   (b) Staircase
(c) Special seeding (d) Seeding

Ans. *(b)* Staircase

5. In a double league tournament such as the IPL, a total of how many matches are played during the league phase if 7 teams participate?
(a) 42   (b) 45
(c) 54   (d) 58

Ans. *(a)* 42

6. In a single knockout tournament, how many byes need to be given if 17 teams are participating?
(a) 17   (b) 16
(c) 15   (d) 14

Ans. *(c)* 15

☑ 1 Mark Questions (VSA)

1. What is planning in games and sports?
or What do you mean by 'Planning in Sports'?
CBSE 2019, CBSE (C) 2018

Ans. Planning in sports is required because there is a definite time frame for achieving the objectives and the results are also known very clearly and in definite terms. Thus, planning is necessary in sports for management of tournaments, formation of different committees for sports events, organisation of intramural and extramural activities, planning various types of fixtures in sports tournaments, ensuring wide participation etc.

2. What do you mean by fixture? **CBSE 2018**

Ans. Fixture is the process of arranging the teams in systematic order in various groups for competition in a physical activity.

In other words, it is the setup of various teams for competitive matches where they play in a systematic order as per the fixture schedule. The success of a tournament depends upon planning of suitable fixtures.

3. What is bye? **All India 2016, 2014**

Ans. Bye is a privilege given to a team which is decided generally by seeding it or by draw of lots.

4. Write formula for giving bye. **All India 2016**

Ans. Formula for giving bye
= Next higher power of 2 − No. of Teams

$$\text{Upper Half} = \frac{Nb-1}{2}, \qquad \text{Lower Half} = \frac{Nb+1}{2}$$

where Nb = total number of byes

5. Explain procedure for giving bye.
CBSE 2013, 2012

Ans. Byes can be applied equally to single person competitions and team sports as well as to single game eliminations and best of series eliminations. If the number of competitors or competing teams are not a multiple of 2 then some teams may get 'bye.'

6. What is seeding? **CBSE 2013, 2011**

Ans. Seeding is a procedure by which good teams are placed in fixtures in such a way that stronger teams do not meet each other at the very start of a tournament. In seeding, the strong teams are selected to keep them at appropriate places in the fixtures so that they should not meet in the earlier rounds.

7. Mention any two responsibilities of the post-meet committees.

Ans. The responsibilities of post-meet committiees are as follows-

(*i*) To check that the outstanding billsare paid.

(*ii*) To reteare press and media news related to the event.

8. What does the school intend by stating that, "only such students shall participate in the Basketball Intramurals who have not represented the school in Basketball in the past and minimum 10 substitutions shall be compulsory?"

Ans. The school's intention is to promote mass participation and to explore the hidden talent of the students.

☑ 3 Marks Questions

1. Write the name of various committees.
All India 2016

Ans. Arrangement Committee, Technical Committee, Discipline Committee, Reception Committee, Boarding and Lodging Committees, Certificate Writing Committee, Medical Committee, Announcement Committee, Recorders and Bulletin Board Committee.

2. What do you mean by knock-out tournament? Draw the fixture of 21 teams on knock-out basis. **CBSE 2016, 2014, 2013**

Ans. In knock-out tournament, the team which is defeated once gets eliminated immediately and will not be given another chance to play. The total number of matches to be played in this tournament will be equal to the number of teams participating minus one $(N-1)$, e.g. if 21 teams are participating, the total number of matches will be $21-1=20$.

Number of teams in upper half

$$= \frac{N+1}{2} = \frac{21+1}{2} = 11$$

Number of teams in lower half

$$= \frac{N-1}{2} = \frac{21-1}{2} = 10$$

Total number of byes

= Next higher power of two − total teams

= $32 - 21 = 11$ byes

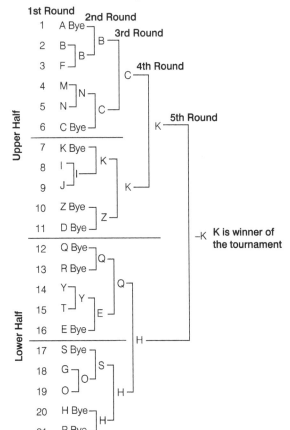

3. Draw a fixture of 11 Football teams participating in a tournament on the basis of knock-out. **All India 2016**

Ans. Total number of teams = 11

$$\text{Upper half} = \frac{N+1}{2} = \frac{11+1}{2} = 6$$

$$\text{Lower half} = \frac{N-1}{2} = \frac{11-1}{2} = 5$$

No. of Byes = Next power of two − of teams

$$= 16 - 11 = 5$$

$$\text{No. of Byes in Lower Half} = \frac{Nb+1}{2} = \frac{5+1}{2} = 3$$

$$\text{No. of Byes in Upper Half} = \frac{Nb-1}{2} \simeq = \frac{5-1}{2} = 2$$

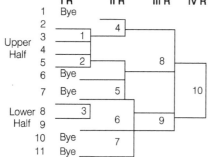

4. Draw the fixture of 7 teams on knock-out basis.

Ans. Total number of matches = $N - 1 = 7 - 1 = 6$

Fixture

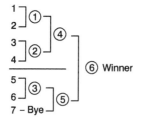

Number of teams in upper half

$$= \frac{N+1}{2} = \frac{7+1}{2} = \frac{8}{2} = 4 \text{ teams}$$

Number of teams in lower half

$$= \frac{N-1}{2} = \frac{7-1}{2} = \frac{6}{2} = 3 \text{ teams}$$

Total number of byes = Next higher power of two − Total teams = 8 − 7 = 1 bye

5. Explain the staircase method of a league tournament for 7 teams.

Ans. In staircase method, fixtures are made similar to a ladder or staircase. This method is the easiest method because no bye is given to any team and there is no need of the stipulation of odd or even number of teams.

1 - 2					
1 - 3	2 - 3				
1 - 4	2 - 4	3 - 4			
1 - 5	2 - 5	3 - 5	4 - 5		
1 - 6	2 - 6	3 - 6	4 - 6	5 - 6	
1 - 7	2 - 7	3 - 7	4 - 7	5 - 7	6 - 7

$$\text{Total matches} = \frac{N(N-1)}{2} = \frac{7(7-1)}{2}$$

$$= \frac{7 \times 6}{2} = \frac{42}{2} = 21 \text{ matches}$$

6. Explain cyclic method of league tournament for 4 teams.

Ans. In this method, one team is kept fixed and the other teams are moved clockwise. When the number of teams is even, no bye is given, but if the number of teams is odd, one bye is given in each round.

Round I

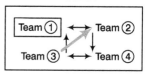

Round II

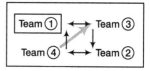

Round III

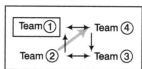

$$\text{Total matches} = \frac{N(N-1)}{2} = \frac{4(4-1)}{2} = \frac{4 \times 3}{2} = \frac{12}{2} = 6$$

(2 matches in each round) in which team 1 is fixed.

⬚ 5 Marks Questions

1. Mention all calculations and steps involved to draw a Knock-out fixture of 19 teams, where 4 teams are to be seeded. **CBSE 2018**

Ans. Knock-out or Elimination Tournaments (also called an Olympic System Tournament) is a type of elimination tournament where the loser of each bracket is immediately eliminated from the tournament.

A fixture of 19 teams on knock-out basis is as follows

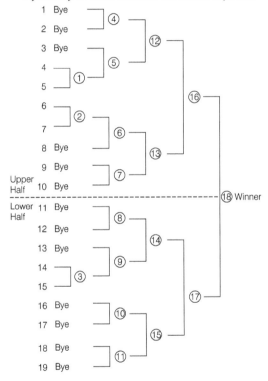

2. Draw a knock-out fixture of 27 teams and explain the advantage of knock out tournament. **CBSE (C) 2018**

or What is the meaning of tournament? Draw knock-out fixture for 27 teams. **CBSE 2012**

Ans. A tournament is a competition held among various teams in a particular activity according to a fixed schedule in which a winner is decided.

	I Round	II Round	III Round Quarter Final	IV Round Semi Final	V Round Final
1	Bye				
2	Bye	12			
3	1		20		
4					
5	2	13			
6					
7	3			24	
8		14			
9	4				
10					
11	5		21		
12		15			
13	6				26
14					
15	Bye	16			
16	Bye				
17	7		22		
18					
19	8	17			
20					
21	9			25	
22		18			
23	10				
24			23		
25	11				
26		19			
27	Bye				

Total no. of teams　　　= 27
Total no. of matches　= 27 − 1 = 26
Number of teams in upper half = $\dfrac{N + 1}{2}$

$$= \dfrac{27 + 1}{2} = 14$$

Number of teams in lower half

$$= \dfrac{N - 1}{2} = \dfrac{27 - 1}{2} = 13$$

Total no. of byes　　　= 32 − 27 = 5
Number of byes in upper half = $\dfrac{5 - 1}{2} = 2$

Number of byes in lower half = $\dfrac{5 + 1}{2} = 3$

Advantages of Knock-Out Tournament

The advantage of knock-out tournament are

(i) Minimum number of officials are required to organise such tournaments.

(ii) Less number of matches are required; thus it require less time to complete such tournaments.

(iii) It is less expensive because the team which gets defeated is eliminated from the competition.

3. Being sports captain of the school, prepare five important committees with their responsibilities to conduct one day run for health race. **Delhi 2015**

Ans. Being the sports captain, I will form five committees. *These are as follows*

(*i*) **Publicity Committee** This committee will prepare the advertisement plans, announce the sports events dates, venues and notify the same to public through newspaper, television, e-mail and websites.

(*ii*) **Boarding and Lodging Committee** This committee will arrange the accommodation of the participants and ensure the provisions for food and refreshments.

(*iii*) **Transportation Committee** This committee provides the necessary transportation to the participants to and fro the venue.

(*iv*) **Grounds and Equipments Committee** This committee takes care of the ground where the event is to take place. At the same time, it also takes care of the equipment and check if they are running properly.

(*v*) **Reception Committee** The members of this committee are responsible to welcome the Chief Guest and spectators at opening and closing ceremonies.

4. Draw a knock-out fixture of 21 teams mentioning all the steps involved. **All India 2015**

Ans. Total no. of matches $= N - 1 = 21 - 1 = 20$

∴ No. of teams in upper half
$$= \frac{N + 1}{2} = \frac{21 + 1}{2}$$
$$= 11 \text{ teams}$$

No. of teams in lower half
$$= \frac{N - 1}{2} = \frac{21 - 1}{2} = 10 \text{ teams}$$

Total no. of byes $Nb = 32 - 21 = 11$ byes

No. of byes in upper half
$$= \frac{Nb - 1}{2} = \frac{11 - 1}{2} = 5 \text{ byes}$$

No. of byes in lower half
$$= \frac{Nb + 1}{2} = \frac{11 + 1}{2} = 6 \text{ byes}$$

Total rounds $= 5$

No. of byes in I quarter
$$= \frac{Nb - 1}{2} = \frac{5 - 1}{2} = 2 \text{ byes}$$

No. of byes in II quarter
$$= \frac{Nb + 1}{2} = \frac{5 + 1}{2} = 3 \text{ byes}$$

No. of byes in III quarter
$$= \frac{Nb}{2} = \frac{6}{2} = 3 \text{ byes}$$

No. of byes in IV quarter
$$= \frac{Nb}{2} = \frac{6}{2} = 3 \text{ byes}$$

5. Suggest the formation of various committees for systematic and smooth conduct of sports day in your school. **All India 2014**

Ans. (*i*) **Selection of Members** Students who are interested and motivated to take part should be included in the committee.

(*ii*) **Define Tasks Clearly** Next step is to define the tasks of each committee. All the committee members should be given clear guidelines about their task.

(*iii*) **Plan** Plan the entire event properly, looking at each and every aspect of the sports day.

(*iv*) **Establish Goals** Each committee should be clearly told about their goals so that they know what is expected of them.

6. What do you understand by fixture? Draw a fixture of 13 teams in knock-out tournament. **CBSE 2011**

or What do you mean by tournament? Draw a fixture of 13 teams in knock-out tournaments.

Ans. Fixture is the process of arranging the teams in systematic order in various groups for competition in a physical activity. In other words, it is the arrangement of various teams for competitive matches where they play in a systematic order as per the fixture schedule. A tournament is a competition held among various teams in a particular activity according to a fixed schedule in which a winner is decided.

Fixture of 13 teams

Total teams $= 13$

Total matches $= N - 1 = 13 - 1 = 12$ matches

Number of teams in upper half

$$= \frac{N+1}{2} = \frac{13+1}{2} = \frac{14}{2} = 7 \text{ teams}$$

Number of teams in lower half

$$= \frac{N-1}{2} = \frac{13-1}{2} = \frac{12}{2} = 6 \text{ teams}$$

Total number of byes

= Next power of two – total teams

= 16 – 13 = 3 byes

Number of byes in upper half

$$= \frac{\text{Total number of byes} - 1}{2} = \frac{3-1}{2} = \frac{2}{2} = 1 \text{ bye}$$

Number of byes in lower half

$$= \frac{\text{Total number of byes} + 1}{2}$$

$$= \frac{3+1}{2} = \frac{4}{2} = 2 \text{ byes}$$

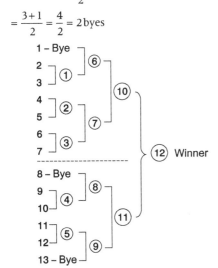

7. While organising sports events for the Annual Sports Day, Arjun and Ravi being the captain and vice captain of sports, formed various committees as shown below. **CBSE QB 2021**

(i) The members of this committee are responsible for welcoming guests and spectators
   (a) Decoration committee
   (b) Reception committee
   (c) Publicity committee
   (d) Transportation committee

(ii) Announcement of venue, date and events is done by ....
   (a) Publicity committee
   (b) Transportation committee
   (c) Ground committee
   (d) Committee for officials

(iii) Organising and conducting of sports events involve ....
   (a) Planning
   (b) Forming committees
   (c) Both (a) and (b)
   (d) Only delegation

(iv) Complete responsibility for success of competition is taken by ....
   (a) Announcement committee
   (b) Administrative director
   (c) First aid committee
   (d) Committee for officials

(v) To prepare a proper score sheet for record is .... responsibility.
   (a) pre tournament
   (b) during tournament
   (c) post tournament
   (d) All of the above

Ans. (i) - (b),   (ii) - (a),   (iii) - (c),   (iv) - (b),   (v) - (b)

CHAPTER 02

Children and Women in Sports

Sports help children develop physical skills, get exercise, make friends, have fun, learn to play as a member of a team, learn to play fair and improve self-esteem. This is because sports or physical activities have a positive influence, provide a sense of accomplishment as a child masters the skills.

Common Postural Deformities

This refers to the deformation in the skeletal structure or where the body parts are not aligned that results in some kind of postural deformities. People having postural deformities cannot perform their work efficiently.

Some common postural deformities are Knock Knee, Flat Foot, Round Shoulders, Lordosis, Kyphosis, Bow Legs and Scoliosis.

1. Knock Knee

Knock knee is a postural deformity in which both the knees touch or overlap each other in the normal standing position. Due to this deformity, an individual usually faces difficulty during walking.

Causes

- Weakness of muscles and ligaments.
- Overweight body.
- Lack of balanced diet.
- Lack of vitamin D, calcium and phosphorus.

Precautions

- Balanced diet should be taken.
- Do not force the babies to walk at early age.

Corrective Measures

- Horse riding is to be done regularly, as it is one of the best exercises for correcting this problem.
- Keep a pillow between your knees whenever possible.
- Perform *Padmasana* and *Gomukhasana*.
- Take nutritious meals.

2. Bow Legs

It is a deformity just the reverse of the knock knee position. In fact, if there is a wide gap between the knees, the deformity can be observed easily when an individual walks or runs.

Causes

- Putting extra weight on leg muscles.
- Lack of balanced diet and deficiency of calcium and phosphorus.
- Improper way of walking.
- Forcing babies to walk at a very early age.

Precautions

- Balanced diet should be taken.
- Do not force the babies to walk at early age.

Corrective Measures

- Never stand for a long time.
- Use vitamin D supplement and a proper balanced diet.
- Walk by bending the toes inward or on the inner edge of the feet.
- Proper massage should be given to the child if this problem is observed early in life.

3. Flat Foot

It is a deformity of the feet. In this deformity, there is no arch in the foot and the foot is completely flat. The individual faces problems in standing, walking, jumping and running.

Causes

- Heaviness of the body.
- Standing for a long time.
- Use of poor quality footwear not having an arch.
- Faulty posture.

Precautions

- Wear shoes of proper shape and size.
- High heeled shoes or walking barefoot for long durations should be avoided.

Corrective Measures

- Walk on heels and toes.
- Pick up marbles with toes.
- Perform *Vajrasana*.
- Walk on wooden staircase.

4. Round Shoulders

It is a postural deformity in which the shoulders become round as they are drawn forward, the head is extended and the chin points forward.

Causes

- Poor posture in work, particularly in a desk job.
- Faulty furniture.
- Wrong habit of standing and sitting.
- Carrying heavy load on shoulders.

Precautions

- Do not sit, stand or walk in bent position.
- Avoid tight fitting clothes.

Corrective Measures

- Stand in correct posture.
- Keep the finger tips on your shoulders and encircle your elbows in clockwise and anti-clockwise direction.
- Perform *Chakrasana* and *Dhanurasana* for some time.
- Hold the horizontal bar for some time.

5. Lordosis

It is the inward curvature of the spine or a deformity of spinal curvature. It is an increased forward curve in the lumbar region. It creates problems in standing and walking.

Causes

- Habitual over-eating.
- Improper environment.
- Diseases affecting vertebrae.
- Improper development of muscles.
- Lack of exercise.

Precautions

- Take a balanced diet.
- Keep the body straight while carrying weights.
- Avoid walking too long with weight on one hand.
- Don't walk, sit or stand in bent position.

Corrective Measures

- Perform *Halasana* and *Paschimottasana*.
- Do sit-ups slowly.
- Stand to attention and touch the feet with the hands repeatedly.
- Lie on your back and lift feet vertically.

6. Kyphosis

It is a deformity of the spinal curvature in which there is an increase of exaggeration of a backward curve or a decrease of a forward curve. It is also called as round upper back.

Causes

- Malnutrition, illness.
- Carrying heavy load on shoulders.
- Habit of bending while walking.
- Wearing light and shapeless clothes.

Precautions

- Take a balanced diet.
- Keep the body straight while carrying weights.
- Avoid walking too long with weight on one hand.
- Don't walk, sit or stand in bent position.

Corrective Measures

- Bend head backwards in standing position.
- Perform *Chakrasana* and *Bhujangasana*.
- Hold arms at shoulder level and bending elbows.

7. Scoliosis

It is a postural deformity of spinal curvature in which there is one large lateral curve extending through the whole length of the spine, or there may be two curves. This type of deformity is also called **curve**.

Causes

- Short leg of one side.
- One side flat foot.
- Carrying heavy loads on one shoulder.
- Heredity defects.
- One side paralysis of spinal muscles.

Precautions

- Take a balanced diet.
- Keep the body straight while carrying weights.
- Avoid walking too long with weight on one hand.
- Don't walk, sit or stand in bent position.

Corrective Measures

- Perform *Trikonasana* with proper technique.
- Avoid walking with a heavy weight.

- Lie down in prone position, i.e. on the chest. Right arm should be upward and left arm at side. After that move right arm towards the left overhead. Press down with left hand and then slide the left hip up.
- Stand erect, lift left heel and left hip, extend right arm in an arch and press left hand against the ribs.

Note : This problem can be controlled by an expert doctor.

Special Considerations

Special care should be taken by sportswomen because of the problems associated with their physiology. *Problems faced by women during their life are*

Menarche

Menarche is a girl's first menstrual period. It can happen as early as age 9 or upto age 15. During this time, girls feel tense and emotional. So special attention should be given to them at this time. As a sportsperson, a young woman has to take special care of herself at that time.

Menstrual Dysfunction

Due to participation of women in physical fitness and competitive endurance sports, the incidence of menstrual dysfunction has increased. Long distance running and other sports may lead to alterations in androgen, estrogen and progesterone hormones, which in some women may directly or indirectly result in amenorrhea (absence of menstrual periods) or infertility.

Female Athlete Triad

The 'female athlete triad' is a syndrome of three related conditions generally seen in teenage or adult female athletes who aren't meeting their energy requirements, which ultimately leaves them undernourished. This also affects their performance severely.

The three components of the female athlete triad include

(*i*) **Osteoporosis** It is a condition in which bones become weak and brittle. It occurs when the body loses too much bone, makes too little bones or both.

(*ii*) **Amenorrhea** It is the absence of menstruation periods that can happen for many reasons. Main causes are genetic abnormalities, excessive exercise and extreme physical or psychological stress.

(*iii*) **Eating Disorders** It refers to either eating in excessive amounts or eating in very little amounts. This disorder is related to mental illness and affects a person's physical and mental health.

A female athlete can have one, two, or all three parts of the triad.

Previous Years'

Examination & Other Important Questions

☑ 1 Mark Questions (MCQ)

1. In bow-legs, there is/are : **CBSE 2020**
(a) wide gap between the knees
(b) plain foot sole
(c) knees colliding with each other
(d) both legs curving inwards

Ans. (*a*) wide gap between the knees

2. Abnormal curve of the spine at the front is called : **CBSE 2020**
(a) Scoliosis   (b) Kyphosis
(c) Lordosis   (d) Psoriasis

Ans. (*c*) Lordosis

3. The precaution of .... should be followed if you have the postural deformity of round shoulders.
(a) avoiding wearing of tight-fitting clothes
(b) keeping the body straight while carrying weights
(c) taking a balanced diet
(d) not putting extra weight on the leg muscles

Ans. (*a*) avoiding wearing of tight-fitting clothes

4. Which of the following procedures is not a cause of flat foot?
(a) Lack of vitamin D and calcium
(b) Body heaviness
(c) Faulty posture
(d) Standing for a long time

Ans. (*a*) Lack of vitamin D and calcium

5. The corrective measures for Lordosis include ....
(a) performing *Chakrasana*
(b) performing *Paschimottasana*
(c) Bending the head backwards while standing
(d) All of the above

Ans. (*b*) performing *Paschimottasana*

6. Scoliosis may occur due to ....
(a) paralysis of spinal muscles on one side
(b) one leg being short in length
(c) Carrying heavy loads on one shoulder
(d) Any of the above

Ans. (*d*) Any of the above

7. Which of the following is not a corrective measure for the postural deformity of knock knee?
(a) Keeping a pillow between the knees as much as possible
(b) Not standing for a long time
(c) Performing *Padmasana* and *Gomukhasana*
(d) Regular horse riding

Ans. (*b*) Not standing for a long time

8. Which of the following is a cause of Kyphosis?
(a) Disease affecting vertebrae
(b) Habitual overeating
(c) Wearing light and shapeless clothes
(d) None of the above

Ans. (*c*) Wearing light and shapeless clothes

9. Menstrual dysfunction occurs due to ....
   (a) Amenorrhea
   (b) alterations in androgen, estrogen and progesterone hormones
   (c) participation of women in sports
   (d) None of the above

Ans. *(b)* alterations in androgen, estrogen and progesterone hormones

10. Anorexia can be treated successfully through ....
   (a) medication
   (b) individual psychotherapy
   (c) providing a balanced diet
   (d) All of the above

Ans. *(b)* individual psychotherapy

11. The eating disorder called .... involves binging on food followed by forced vomiting.
   (a) Anorexia
   (b) Amenorrhea
   (c) Bulimia
   (d) None of the above

Ans. *(c)* Bulimia

12. Which of the following components of the female athletes' triad is covered by absence of menstrual periods?
   (a) Amenorrhea
   (b) Osteoporosis
   (c) Disordered eating
   (d) All of the above

Ans. *(a)* Amenorrhea

⬚ 1 Mark Questions (VSA)

1. Which type of deformity is 'Kyphosis'? **CBSE 2019**

Ans. Kyphosis is a deformity of the spine in which there is an increase of exaggeration of a backward curve or a decrease of a forward curve. It is also called as round upper back.

2. What are the causes of Oestoporosis? **CBSE 2019**

or Write in brief about osteoporosis. What are the causes of osteoporosis in women? **All India 2017**

or What is osteoporosis? **All India 2016**

Ans. Osteoporosis is a weakening of the bones due to the loss of bone density and improper bone formation.

Causes of osteoporosis in women are harmonal changes occurring during menopause, lack of calcium and vitamin D in diet, etc.

3. Among females, what type of Menstrual Dysfunction is called Amenorrhoea? **CBSE 2019**

or What is 'Amenorrhoea' in female athletes triad? **CBSE 2018**

Ans. Amenorrhoea is a condition in which there is absence of menstrual periods or they become irregular. It is associated with women athletes because they do intensive exercises which is not followed by taking enough calories. This leads to hormonal imbalances which may cause amenorrhoea.

4. What do you mean by 'Bulimia'? **CBSE 2019**

Ans. Bulimia is a type of eating disorder in which the affected person will eat a large amount of food in a short time (i.e. binge) and then do something to get rid of the food eaten (i.e. purge). They may vomit, exercise too much, or use laxatives.

5. What is female athlete triad? **CBSE (C) 2018**

Ans. The female athlete triad is a syndrome of three related conditions generally observed in teenage or adult female athletes who are not meeting their energy requirements. As a result, they are undernourished. The three components of the female athlete triad are eating disorders, Amenorrhea and Osteoporosis.

6. Name any two postural deformities. **CBSE 2018**

or State the common postural deformities. **All India 2017**

Ans. Common postural deformities are Kyphosis, Flat foot, Knock knee, Lordosis and Bow legs.

7. What are the causes of knock knee?

Ans. *The causes of knock knee are*
   • Weakness of muscles and ligaments
   • Overweight body
   • Lack of balanced diet
   • Lack of vitamin D, calcium and phosphorus

8. What do you mean by menarche?

Ans. A girl's first menstrual period is known as menarche. Girls may face stress and emotional tension during menarche. Menarche usually occurs between 9 or upto 15 years of age.

☑ 3 Marks Questions

1. Write briefly about the prevention and management of "Anorexia". **CBSE 2019**

Ans. Anorexia can be prevented by children developing healthy eating habits and a strong body image from an early age. They should not develop cultural values that consider 'thin' as perfect bodies. They should be told about the side effects of malnourishment and the life threatening nature of anorexia.

Management of Anorexia can be accomplished by

   (*i*) **Facing Reality** This is essential, as the affected person must admit that she has a problem of Anorexia and the relentless pursuit of thinness is out of her control.

   (*ii*) **Restoring Healthy Weight** An affected person cannot recover from Anorexia without restoring appropriate body weight. A psychologist can play an effective role in helping the person to return to a healthy weight. A dietician can provide adequate and proper guidance for a healthy diet for full recovery.

2. Write about the deformities of spinal curvature. **All India 2016**

Ans. There are three types of spinal curvature

   (*i*) **Lordosis** It is the inward curvature of the spine or a deformity of spinal curvature. It is an increased forward curve in the lumbar region. It creates problems in standing and walking.

   (*ii*) **Kyphosis** It is a deformity of the spinal curvature in which there is an increase of exaggeration of a backward curve or a decrease of a forward curve. It is also called round upper back.

   (*iii*) **Scoliosis** It is a postural deformity of spinal curvature in which there is one large lateral curve extending through the whole length of the spine, or there may be two curves. This type of deformity is also called curve.

3. Suggest exercises as corrective measures for round shoulders. **Delhi 2014**

Ans. Round shoulders is a postural deformity in which the shoulders become round as they are drawn forward, the head is extended and the chin points forward. *The corrective measures are*

   • Stand in correct posture.

   • Keep the finger tips on your shoulders and encircle your elbows in clockwise and anti-clockwise direction.

   • Perform *Chakrasana* and *Dhanurasana* for some time.

   • Hold the horizontal bar for some time.

4. What are the causes of menstrual dysfunction?

Ans. Due to participation of women in physical fitness and competitive endurance sports, the incidence of menstrual dysfunction has increased. Long distance running and other sports may lead to alterations in androgen, estrogen and progesterone hormones, which in some women may directly or indirectly result in amenorrhea (absence of menstrual periods) or infertility.

5. What do you understand by female athlete triad and what are its components?

Ans. The 'female athlete triad' is a syndrome of three related conditions generally seen in teenage or adult female athletes who aren't meeting their energy requirements, which ultimately leaves them undernourished.

The three components of the female athlete triad include

   (*i*) Disordered eating and anaemia (Energy deficits)

   (*ii*) Osteoporosis (Decreased bone density)

   (*iii*) Amenorrhea (Menstrual irregularities)

6. Mahesh, Physical Education teacher at XYZ School observed that Raju a student of class VI has outward curve of vertebral column at Thoracic region. He suggested some exercises to rectify this problem.

   (i) What is this deformity known as?
      (a) Scoliosis
      (b) Kyphosis
      (c) Lordosis
      (d) Flat foot

   (ii) Kyphosis is commonly known as
      (a) Hollow back
      (b) Hunch back
      (c) Sideways bending
      (d) Lordosis

   (iii) Kyphosis is a deformity related to
      (a) Foot   (b) Vertebral column
      (c) Shoulder   (d) Legs

Ans. (i) - (b),   (ii) - (b),   (iii) - (b)

☑ 5 Marks Questions

1. Explain 'Flat Foot' and 'Knock Knees' and also suggest corrective measures for both postural deformities. **CBSE 2019**

Ans. Flat Foot is a deformity of the feet. In this deformity, there is no arch in the foot, so that the foot is completely flat. Thus, the affected individual faces problems in standing, walking, jumping and running.

Corrective measures for this deformity are
  (*i*) Walk on heels and toes.
  (*ii*) Pick up marbles with toes.
  (*ii*) Slowly write the alphabet using marbles.
  (iv) Perform *Vajrasan* regularly.
  (iv) Walk on wooden staircase.

Knock Knees is a postural deformity in which both the knees touch or overlap each other in the normal standing position. Due to this deformity, an individual usually faces difficulty during walking.

Corrective measures for this deformity are
  (*i*) Horse riding is to be done regularly.
  (*ii*) Perform *Padmasana* and *Gomukhasana* regularly.
  (*iii*) Keep a pillow between the knees whenever possible.
  (*iv*) Be careful while you walk and stand.
  (*iv*) Take nutritious meals.

2. Suggest five exercises as corrective measures for Round shoulders and Kyphosis. **CBSE (C) 2018**

Ans. *Five exercises suggested for Kyphosis and Round shoulders are*
  (*i*) Perform *Chakrasana* (for both problems), *Bhujangasana* (for Kyphosis) and *Dhanurasana* (for Round shoulders).
  (*ii*) For Round shoulders, while keeping your finger tips on your shoulders, move your elbows in circular motion clockwise and anti-clockwise alternately.
  (*iii*) For Round shoulders, hold the horizontal bar for some time with both hands.
  (*iv*) For Kyphosis, hold the arms at shoulder level and bend the elbows.
  (*v*) For Kyphosis, bend the head backwards in standing position.

3. Mention the causes, precautions and corrective measures of knock knees. **CBSE 2012**

Ans. *Causes*
  * Weakness of muscles and ligaments.
  * Lack of balanced diet.
  * Lack of vitamin D, calcium and phosphorus.
  * Overweight body.

Precautions
  * Balanced diet should be taken.
  * Do not force the babies to walk at early age.

Corrective Measures
  * Horse riding is to be done regularly.
  * Keep a pillow between your knees whenever possible.
  * Perform *Padmasana* and *Gomukhasana*.
  * Take nutritious meals.

4. Explain any five common postural deformities.

Ans. *Five common postural deformities are*
  (*i*) **Knock Knee** It is a postural deformity in which both the knees touch or overlap each other in normal standing position.
  (*ii*) **Flat Foot** It is a deformity of the feet. In this deformity, there is no arch in the foot and the foot is completely flat.
  (*iii*) **Round Shoulder** It is a postural deformity in which the shoulders become round as they are drawn forward, the head is extended with the chin pointing forward.
  (*iv*) **Kyphosis** It is a deformity of the spinal curvature in which there is an increase or exaggeration of a backward curve.
  (*v*) **Bow Legs** It is a deformity opposite to knock knee. In fact, if there is a wide gap between the knees, the deformity can be observed easily when an individual walks or runs.

5. What do you understand by the female athlete triad? Explain the symptoms and causes of any one of them.

Ans. Refer to Q. No. 5 (3 Marks Questions) on page no. 19.

Amenorrhea refers to the absence of menstrual periods. The periods may have stopped, become irregular or never occurred. There are many reasons responsible for amenorrhea including extensive exercise and improper diet. Exercising intensively and not consuming enough calories can lead to harmonal imbalances that result in a girl's periods becoming irregular or stopping altogether.

6. Sheethal spent her weekend checking the health status of all the security guards of her huge gated community as a part of project work assigned by PE teachers. She found out that more than half of them have shown a significant deformity in the upper part of their vertebral column.
CBSE QB 2021

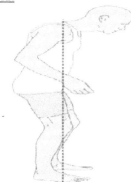

(i) The term used to define this deformity is ....
    (a) Lordosis   (b) Scoliosis
    (c) Kyphosis   (d) Both (a) and (b)

(ii) This deformity is mainly caused due to ....
    (a) carrying heavy loads
    (b) lack of exercise
    (c) weak muscles
    (d) All of the above

(iii) The asana/s which helps in rectifying such condition/sis/are ....
    (a) Chakrasana   (b) Dhanurasana
    (c) Halasana   (d) Both (a) and (b)

(iv) Bending head backward in standing position helps in getting rid of ....
    (a) Lordosis
    (b) Kyphosis
    (c) Scoliosis
    (d) Both (a) and (b)

(v) Due to Covid Pandemic, most of the children attending online classes with bad sitting posture may experience this condition later
    (a) Kyphosis   (b) Lordosis
    (c) Scoliosis   (d) Flat foot

Ans. (i) - (c),   (ii) - (d),   (iii) - (d),   (iv) - (a),   (v) - (a)

7. Posture plays a very significant role in our daily activities. Correct posture means the balancing of body in accurate and proper manner. Various types of postural deformities can be identified in individuals. **CBSE QB 2021**

(i) From the above given picture, the deformities seen on the left most is caused due to deficiency of ....
    (a) Iron   (b) Calcium
    (c) Vit-D   (d) Both (b) and (c)

(ii) Walking on the inner edge of the feet can be a remedy for ....
    (a) Bow legs   (b) Flat foot
    (c) Overweight   (d) Leg deformity

(iii) The person in the middle is suffering with ....
    (a) Rickets   (b) Flatfoot
    (c) Knock knees   (d) Elephant foot

(iv) Horse-riding is the best exercise for clearing this deformity
    (a) Knock knees   (b) Bow legs
    (c) Flat foot   (d) All of these

(v) Performing this asana regularly can be a remedy for Knock-knees
    (a) Padmasana   (b) Tadasana
    (c) Vajrasana   (d) Halasana

Ans. (i) - (d),   (ii) - (a),   (iii) - (c),   (iv) - (a),   (v) - (a)

CHAPTER 03

Yoga and Lifestyle

Yoga as a lifestyle or the 'yogic way' has become very much accepted to keep healthy. It is amazing that a more than 5000 year old lifestyle tradition has become a popular way of life. The power of yoga is in its simplicity, diversity and flexibility. It is an ancient science which harmonises the body, mind and spirit. The word 'yoga' is derived from the Sanskrit word 'Yuj' which means 'to join'. To Patanjali, the founder of yoga, the word 'yuj' is to stabilise the mind for the union of our soul (*Atma*) with God (*Parmatama*).

According to the *Gita* (epic book), Yoga is "evenness of temper."

According to Swami Digambar Ji, "Yoga is a union of *Atma* and *Parmatama*."

According to Shankracharya, "Yoga is withdrawal of the sense organs from worldly objects and their control through yoga."

Obesity

Excess weight or deposition of excess fats in the body is called obesity. It leads to various diseases such as diabetes, heart disease, hypertension, lowered pulmonary function, less life expectancy etc. Obesity is a condition in which the Body Mass Index (BMI) is higher than 30.

There are various reasons for obesity such as lack of proper exercise, poor eating habits, psychological factors, endocrine gland problems, familial tendency etc. Males are at high risk of obesity between the ages of 29 and 35, whereas females are at high risk between the ages of 45 and 49.

The risk increases with age thereafter. Various asanas can be practised effectively to reduce body weight, control obesity and achieve a normal healthy condition of body and mind. The major asanas which should be practised to control obesity are Tadasana, Katichakrasana, Ardh Matsyendrasana etc.

Tadasana (Mountain Pose)

Procedure

- This is done in standing position.
- Stand straight and join the feet together.
- Toes must touch each other and heels may be slightly apart.
- With deep inhalation, raise up both the arms and then interlock the fingers.
- Stretch your shoulders and chest upward.
- Hold for 4 to 8 breaths.
- Exhale and drop the shoulders down.

Benefits

- It improves body posture and reduces flat feet problem.
- Knees, thighs and ankles become stronger.
- Buttocks and abdomen get toned.
- It helps to alleviate sciatica.
- It also makes spine more agile.
- It helps in increasing height and improves balance.
- It regulates digestive, nervous and respiratory systems.

Contraindications

- Avoid during headaches or insomnia.
- Avoid during low blood pressure.

Katichakrasana

Procedure

- Stand up straight with your feet together.
- Keep your spine erect keep the shoulders straight.
- Keep your legs apart from each other equivalent to the shoulders.
- Stretch your hands to the front, palms facing each other.
- Your hands should be in line with the shoulders.
- First inhale and then while exhaling twist from the waist to the right and look back over the right.
- Keep your breath out and stay in this position as long as possible.
- Inhale and slowly come back to the center.
- Exhale and twist from the waist to the left and look back over the left.
- Keep your breath out.
- Stay in this final posture as long as possible.
- Come back to the center and relax.
- In the twisted position if you want to stay for longer then you need slowly keep on breathing.
- This is the complete cycle of this posture.
- Practice can be repeated 10 to 20 times or even more than that as per the convenience.

Benefits

- It helps to remove lethargy.
- It improves the flexibility of the spine and waist.
- It strengthens the spine and waist.
- It is good for relieving constipation.
- It opens up the neck and shoulders.
- It provides a stretch in different muscles of arm, abdomen and legs.
- It helps to relieve back pain.

Contraindications

- Katichakrasana should not be practised by those who have recently undergone any abdomen or spinal surgery.
- It should be avoided by persons suffering from hernia, slip disc or any abdominal inflammation.
- It should be avoided during pregnancy.

Pavanamuktasana

Procedure

- This is done in lying position.
- Lie flat on the back, keep the legs straight and relax your body.
- Inhale slowly and lift the legs and bend on the knees. Bring upwards to the chest till the thigh touches the stomach.
- Hug the knees and lock the fingers.
- Place the nose tip between the knees.
- Exhale slowly and come back to the original position.

Benefits

- It cures acidity, indigestion and constipation.
- It is helpful for those suffering from gastrointestinal problems, arthritis, heart problems and waist and back pain.
- This is very beneficial for stomach abs. The results are very impressive.
- It strengthens back muscle and cures back pain.
- It is very beneficial for reproductive organs and for menstruation disorder.

Contraindications

- Those who are suffering from high blood pressure, hernia, heart problems and ulcer should avoid.
- During pregnancy and menstruation, women should avoid it.

Matsyasana (Fish Pose)

Procedure

- This asana is done in lying pose.
- Lift your hips and tuck your hands slightly beneath your buttocks, palms facing down. Draw your forearms and elbows in towards your body.

- With inhale, bend your elbows and press firmly on your forearms and elbows to lift your head and upper body away from the floor.
- Firm your shoulder blades into your back and lift your chest higher towards the ceiling, elongate your spine.
- Bring the crown of your head down on the floor, placing a minimal amount of weight on your head.
- Remain here with your knees bent, or, if it feels uncomfortable, extend both legs straight down on the mat in front of you with your muscles strongly engaged.
- Stay in the pose anywhere from 5 to 10 deep breaths.

Benefits

- It stretches the neck muscles and shoulders.
- This pose provides relief from respiratory disorders by encouraging deep breathing, as this pose increases lung capacity to a great extent.
- There is an increased supply of blood to the cervical and thoracic regions of the back that helps tone the parathyroid, pituitary and pineal glands.
- This pose helps to regulate emotions and stress.
- The practice of Matsyasana brings down the tension and the stiffness at the neck and the shoulders.

Contraindications

- Individuals suffering from high or low blood pressure should avoid this posture.
- Women who are pregnant should not attempt this yoga pose.
- Injury in neck or any part of the lower back or middle back can make it difficult to practice this fish pose and hence should be avoided.

Halasana (Plow Pose)
Procedure

- Lie on the yoga mat or carpet and join the legs together.

- Raise your legs to make an angle of 90 degrees.
- Thrust the palms, raise the waist and legs, bending forwards curving the back and resting the legs on the floor above head.Try to place the big toe on the floor and keep the legs straight.
- Balance the whole weight on the shoulder blade, shift both the hands over the head, join the fingers and hold the head with it and relax the elbows on the floor.
- Try to remain in the position till the count of 100.
- Then release the fingers above the head, pressing the palms on the floor taking back thumb toe gently bring the body and legs to the floor.
- Relax in corpse pose and practice for 2 more rounds.

Benefits

- Practicing this asana regularly can avoid disease like diabetes, obesity, constipation, stomach disorder, blood pressure and menstrual disorders.
- It makes your backbone elastic and flexible.
- It helps to reduce both belly and body fat.
- It improves memory power.

Contraindications

- It should be avoided by those having neck pain, spondylosis, and high blood pressure should not practice this yoga pose.
- It should be avoided by pregnant women.

Paschimottanasana
Procedure

- This is done in sitting posture.
- Sit on the floor with the legs stretched out.
- Sit straight, raise both arms above your head and stretch up.
- Bend forwards and hold the big toes with the middle and index fingers.
- Then, exhale out slowly and try to touch the knees with your forehead.
- Stay in this position for five deep breaths and relax the muscles while exhale.

Benefits

- It stretches hamstrings, spine, shoulders and hip joints.
- It enhances secretion of insulin from pancreas and improves digestion.
- It relieves menstrual discomfort and enhances fertility.
- It reduces headache, anxiety, insomnia and sinusitis.
- It reduces abdominal fats and increases metabolism.
- It helps in controlling constipation.

Contraindications

- Pregnant women should avoid this asana.
- It should be avoided by person suffering from respiratory and spinal problem.
- Ulcer patient should also avoid this asana.

Ardha Matsyendrasana (Half Spinal Twist Pose)

Procedure

- This is done in sitting posture.
- Sit with legs straight and stretched in front of you.
- Bend the left leg and bring it close to the body. Place it under the right buttocks.
- Then, place the right leg next to the left knee by taking it over the knee.
- Twist your waist, neck and shoulders over your right shoulder. While doing it, keep your spine straight.
- Place the right hand behind and the left hand on the right knee.
- Breathe normally and slowly in this position.
- Repeat with the other leg.

Benefits

- It is one of the best poses to improve the flexibility of the spine. It energises the spine.
- It improves functioning of liver and kidneys.
- It stretches the shoulders, hips and neck. It stimulates the digestive enzymes in the belly.

- It relieves menstrual discomfort, fatigue, sciatica and backache. It is therapeutic for asthma and infertility.

Contraindications

- Avoid during pregnancy and menstruation due to the strong twist in the abdomen.
- People with heart, abdominal or brain surgeries should avoid this asana.
- Those who are having peptic ulcer or hernia should avoid it.
- Those with severe spinal problems should avoid it.
- People with severe slip disc problem should avoid it.

Dhanurasana (Bow Pose)

Procedure

- Lie on your stomach.
- Hold your both feet with your hands making a back bend and positioning like a bow.
- Pull your both feet slowly – slowly, as much as you can.
- Look straight ahead with a smile in your face.
- Keep the pose stable while paying attention to your breath.
- After 1-20 seconds as you exhale,gently bring your legs and chest to the ground and relax.

Benefits

- Dhanurasana strengthens the back and the abdomen at the same time.
- It helps improve upon stomach disorders.
- It also helps in reducing fat around belly area.
- It is beneficial specifically to women as it improves reproductive system and helps improve menstrual disorders.
- It helps to regulate the pancreas and is recommended for people with diabetes.
- It expands the thoracic region of the chest.
- It helps to alleviate hunchback.
- It increases the appetite.

Contraindications

- It should not be practiced by those suffering from high blood pressure, backpain, headache, migraine or abdomen surgery.
- It should not be practiced by women during pregnancy.

Ushtrasana (Camel Pose)

Procedure

- Sit on the floor stretching your leg and keeping your spine erect keeping palms on the ground side by the buttocks.
- Bend your leg by the keens and sit on your heels placing the buttocks between the heels, the right big toe overlapping the left.
- Kneel on floor keeping your knees in line with the shoulders and sole of the feet facing the ceiling.
- Keep your hand on thighs.
- Inhale and arch your back and place your palms on the heels of the feet.
- Keep your arms straight.
- Do not strain your neck keep it neutral. Let your neck be free.
- Stay in this final position for couple of breaths or as much longer as you can.
- Breathe out and slowly come to the normal position withdrawing your hands from the feet.

Benefits

- Ushtrasana stretches the anterior muscles of the body.
- It improves flexibility of spine and strengthens it.
- It improves digestion.
- It gives relaxation to the lower back.
- It is useful as an initial practice for back bending.
- It reduces abdomen fat.

Contraindications

It should not be practiced by people suffering from severe back and neck injury, high or low blood pressure, migraine or other severe headache.

Surya Bhedana Pranayama

Procedure

- Sit comfortably in Padmasana or Siddhasana.
- Keep your head and spine erect with eye closed.
- Shut your left nostril with your ring finger and little finger.
- Now breathe in (inhale) slowly and deeply through your right nadi.
- After that, shut your right nadi with the thumb of your right hand.
- Then exhale through your left nostril, along with keeping your right nostril closed.
- This is one cycle is completed.
- Repeat this process around 5 – 10 times.

Benefits

- It activates the body functions.
- It is very helpful for increasing the digestive fire.
- It cures all diseases that are caused by the insufficiency of oxygen in the blood.
- It destroys intestinal worms.
- It is the best breathing exercise for cold and cough, or other respiratory problems.
- It is a best and simple method in low blood pressure.

Contraindications

Surya Bhedana Pranayama should not to be practiced in case of blocked nostril, hypertension, heart problem, hyperthyroid, anxiety, anger, epilepsy, peptic ulcer or when suffering from external heat boils, fever or constipation.

Diabetes

Diabetes is a disease in which the pancreas fail to produce insulin or is unable to use the insulin produced in an effective manner.

Insulin is a harmone produced by the pancreas that helps glucose, present in the blood, to enter the cells in our body and provide energy.

Insufficient secretion of insulin by pancreas results in excess glucose (sugar level) in the blood stream.

This causes diabetes and damages the organs. It is of two types *viz.* **Type I** and **Type II**. In Type I diabetes, the body is unable to produce insulin and in Type II diabetes, body produces insulin, but unable to use if effectively.

It can lead to renal failure, loss of vision, amputation of limbs and cardiovascular diseases.

Asanas for Diabetes

Asanas like *Katichakrasana, Pavanamuktasana, Bhujangasana, Shalabhasana, Dhanurasana, Supta Vajrasana, Paschimottasana, Ardha Matsyendrasana, Mandukasana, Gomukhasana, Yoga Mudrasana, Ushtrasana and Kapalabhati* can help in preventing and curing diabetes. These are follows

Note *Katichakrasana, Pavanamuktasana, Dhanurasana, Paschimottasana, Ardha Matsyendrasana and Ushtrasana are already described previously in the chapter.*

Bhujangasana (The Cobra Pose)

Procedure

- This is done in lying posture.
- Lie on the stomach and rest forehead on the floor.
- Keep the feet and toes together and touch the ground.
- Place the hands at shoulder level and palms on floor.
- Inhale and lift the head, chest, abdomen up towards roof and keep the navel on the floor.
- Pull your torso back and off the floor with support of your hands.

Benefits

- It improves the blood circulation in body.
- It decreases menstrual irregularities in females.
- It strengthens muscles of chest, shoulders, arms and abdomen.
- It is effective in urine disorder.
- It improves the functioning of reproductive organ.
- It improves the function of liver, kidney, pancreas and gall bladder.

- It helps to lose weight.

Contraindications

- Avoid during pregnancy.
- People having a hernia problem and backache should not do this asana.
- It should be avoided by persons who are suffering from ulcer, heart problem or any surgeries of spine.

Shalabhasana

Procedure

- This is done in lying position. Lie down on the stomach; place both hands underneath the thighs.
- Breathe in (inhale) and lift both the legs upward without bending the knees.
- The chin should rest on the ground.
- Maintain this position for 2-3 minutes for better results.
- Do not put much strain in leg .
- Bring down both legs back to starting position.

Benefits

- It is beneficial for spinal problems.
- It is helpful for backache and sciatica pain.
- It removes unwanted fats around abdomen, waist, hips and thighs.
- It cures cervical spondylitis and spinal cord ailments.
- It helps in strengthening the wrists, hips, thighs, legs, buttocks, lower abdomen and diaphragm.
- It gives flexibility to the back muscles and spine.
- It strengthens the shoulders and neck muscles.

Contraindications

- It should be avoided during headache and serious back injury.
- Person suffering from hernia should avoid it.

Supta Vajrasana (Reclined Thunderbolt Pose)

Procedure

- Sit comfortably in Vajrasana.
- Keeping your palms on the floor beside the buttocks, your fingers pointing to the front.
- Slowly bend back, putting the proper forearm and also the elbow on the bottom so the left.
- Slowly bring down your head to the ground while arching the back. Place your hands on the thighs.
- Try to stay the lower legs connected with the ground. If necessary, separate the knees.
- Make certain that you simply don't seem to be overstraining the muscles and ligaments of the legs.
- Close the eyes and relax the body.
- Breathe deeply and slowly within the final position.
- Release within the reverse order, inhaling and taking the support of the elbows and also the arms raise the top higher than the bottom.
- Then shift the weight on the left arm and elbow by slippery the body, then slowly returning to the beginning position.
- Never leave the ultimate position by straightening the legs first; it's going to dislocate the knee joints.
- Repeat this process for 3 to 5 times and once you master it increase the time for 8 to 10 times.

Benefits

- It tones the spinal nerves, makes the rear versatile and realigns rounded shoulders.
- It enhances courageousness and confidence level within the temperament.
- It is useful for those stricken by respiratory disorder and different respiratory organ ailments.
- It regulates the functioning of the adrenal glands.

- It helps to alleviate disorders of male and feminine procreative organs.
- It helps to eliminate anger, aggression and relax the mind.

Contraindications

People having heart issues, such as blocked arteries, angina or recovering from the bypass surgery should avoid this asana.

Mandukasana (Frog Pose)

Procedure

- Comfortably sit in Vajrasana (thunderbolt pose).
- Close the fists of both hands.
- While clenching the fists press your thumb inside with the fingers.
- While pressing the navel with your both fists exhale and bend forward.
- Hold the breath when you are in the position of bend forward and keep looking straight.
- Stay in this position for some time (hold the position as much as you can), inhale, and come back to the starting position (Vajrasana).
- Repeat this three to four times.

Benefits

- Mandukasana increases the quantity of insulin so it is beneficial for curing diabetes.
- It cures the problems related to stomach.
- It is beneficial in cardiovascular diseases.
- It is useful for flexibility of thighs and legs.
- It reduces extra fat from thighs and hips.
- It improves the functioning of the digestive system and excretory system.
- It cures the pain of ankles, knees and back.

Contraindications

- It should be avoided by pregnant women due to pressure at the lower abdomen.
- It should be avoided by those having any kind of ulcer in the body.

Gomukhasana (Cow Face Pose)

Procedure

- This is done in sitting position.
- Sit straight and stretch both legs together in front.
- Fold right leg at the knee and place it on the ground by the side of the left buttock.
- Bringing the left leg from above the right leg, place it on the ground by the side of the right buttock.
- Fold your left arm and place it behind your back. Then, take your right hand over your right shoulder, and stretch it as much as you can until it reaches your left hand.
- After sometime, return to the original position.
- Change the position of the legs *i.e.* by placing the right knee above and the left knee down and repeat this as much as you can.

Benefits

- It helps in stretching and strengthen the muscles of the ankles, hips and thighs, shoulders, triceps, inner armpits and chest.
- It is helpful in curing of sciatica.
- It improves the functioning of lungs.
- Regular practice can reduce stress and anxiety.

Contraindications

- Those who are suffering from shoulder, knee or back pain should avoid it.
- Pregnant women should avoid it.

Yoga Mudrasana

Procedure

- Sit in Padmasana that is, with your legs crossed and soles facing upward close to the navel, inhale deeply.
- As you exhale, stretch your left arm backward and around your right hip. Grasp the big toe of your left foot with this hand.

- Now, repeat by swinging your right arm backward and stretching to grasp the big toe of your right foot with it.
- Inhale deeply and exhale.
- Bend your trunk forward till your forehead rests against the floor.

Benefits

- It stretches the posterior muscles of the trunk and the neck.
- It improves muscle tone and venous circulation of the spinal column.
- It has favourable effects on the viscera due to deep intra-abdominal compression.
- Its lateral stretch stimulates vital areas of the colon.

Contraindications

- Yoga Mudrasana should be avoided by persons with injury of the neck, shoulders, hips, knee, pelvic girdle and ankles.
- It should be avoided by the persons with back issues related to injury, surgery or pain.

Kapalabhati

Kapala means skull (head) and Bhati means to shine. Because this practice makes the skull (head) shine, therefore it is called Kapalabhati. In other words, it rejuvenates the skull (head) and the mental functions.

Procedure

- Sit in a meditative posture, eyes closed and the whole body relaxed.
- Inhale deeply through both nostrils expanding the abdomen and exhale with a forceful contraction of the abdominal muscles.
- The breathing must be of the 'bellows' type and perform 30-40 strokes in one round. Start from 10 strokes.
- At the end of practice, deep exhale and relax.

Benefits

- It purifies the frontal air sinuses and stimulates the brain.
- Massages abdominal organs and improves digestion.

- It increases the capacity of lungs.
- It is useful in treating cold, rhinitis (inflammation of the mucus membrane of the nose), sinusitis and bronchial infections.

Contraindications

- Stroke should be in rhythmic manner.
- Active exhalation and passive inhalation.
- Don't strain the facial muscles during the practice.
- Avoid performing the practice in the case of high blood pressure, heart diseases and gastric ulcers.

Asanas for Asthma

Asthma is a condition in which a person's airways in the lungs become narrow. Due to narrowness, air flow is obstructed. It creates breathing problem in a person.

It is a long-term inflammatory disease. In this disease, the airways also swell up and produce extra mucus, which enhances breathing problem.

The coughing usually occurs at night or early in the morning. It is more complex from other diseases, as it cannot be cured or treated but its symptons can be controlled.

Note *Tadasana, Bhujangasana, Dhanurasana, Ushtrasana, Kapalabhati, Gomukhasana and Matsyendrasana are already discussed in the chapter previously.*

Urdhva Hastasana
Procedure

- Stand in a Tadasana (Mountain pose). Then, gently raise your hand upward.
- Bring the arms parallel to one another and then without bending the shoulders, bring your arms together over your head.
- Expand the elbows completely and reach upwards. Then slightly slant your head backwards and look at the thumbs.
- Shoulder blades must be pressed firmly on your back.
- Bring your buttock inward by compressing them.

- Keep your feet together and press your heel firmly against the ground.

Benefits

- It stretches the complete body and provides a good massage to the arms, spine, upper and lower back, ankles, hands, shoulders, calf muscles and thighs.
- It enhances the functioning of digestive system and increases the capacity of the lungs.
- This asana helps in improving the blood circulation of the body.
- It helps in enhancing the body postures.
- It helps in alleviating nervousness and sadness along with providing a sense of achievement.
- It helps in tightening the abdomen and helps in easing sciatica.

Contraindications

- Avoid in case of shoulder or neck injuries.
- Avoid if experiencing dizziness while staring upwards and in case of any other medical concerns.

Uttana Mandukasana
Procedure

- Sit in Vajrasana.
- Spread both the knees wide apart while toes remaining together.
- Raise your right arm, fold it and take it backward from above the right shoulder and place the palm below the left shoulder.
- Now fold the left arm similarly and place the palm from above below the right shoulder.
- Maintain the position. While coming back, slowly remove the left arm and then right arm; bring the knees together as in the initial position.

Benefits

- It gives stretch to the throat muscles and nerves and relieves throat pain.
- It gives good stretch to the upper and lower back muscles, makes back muscles flexible and relieves back pain and strain.

- It stretches the elbow joints and hence good for elbow health.
- It strengthens the spine, strengthens all cervical, thoracic and lumbar regions.
- It also stretches the diaphragm effectively and also the chest region. This facilitates easy breathing.
- It improves functional efficiency of pancreas.

Contraindications

- It should be avoided by persons suffering from arthritis, hernia, chronic and severe back problems, knee problems, elbow pain and severe shoulder pain, spinal cord deformities and disabilities of hip joints.
- Women should not practice this asana during pregnancy or during menstruation.

Vakrasana (Half Spinal Twist Pose)

Procedure

- This is done in sitting position. It is simplified form of Ardha Matsyendrasana.
- Sit and stretch the legs straight.
- Fold the right leg. Heel of right leg should touch the left leg's knee.
- Take the right hand to back of the waist by twisting the trunk.
- Bring the left hand close to right knee and place it near the right feet.
- Twist the head and shoulder to right side and look straight to the right shoulder's side.
- Turn the head to the front and return to original position.

Benefits

- It reduces belly fat.
- It improves the function of both spinal cord and nervous system.
- It controls diabetes and strengthens kidneys.
- It helps adrenal gland to function properly.
- It helps to control waist, back pain and chronic back pain.

Contraindications

- It should be avoided by persons suffering from ulcer and enlargement of liver.

- It should be avoided by persons suffering from severe back pain and hernia.

Anuloma Viloma/Nadishodhana Pranayama

Nadishodhana means to purify the nadis. Nadishodhana pranayama is also known as anuloma viloma. Viloma means produced in the reverse order. This variety gets its name from the fact that the nostrils are alternatively used during each inhalation and exhalation in this pranayama.

Procedure

- Sit in any comfortable meditative posture.
- Keep the head and spine erect.
- Close the eyes.
- Pay attention to the breath.
- Place the hands on their respective knees.
- Adopt nasagran mudra of the right hand and jnana mudra of the left hand.
- Close the right nostril with the thumb.
- Inhale through the left nostril and exhale through the right nostril, keeping the respiration rate slow, deep and silent.
- Inhale through the right nostril again.
- Exhale through the left nostril, keeping the respiration rate slow, deep and silent.

Benefits

- Calms and steadies the mind, improves focus and concentration.
- Improves blood supply to the brain.
- Balances the left and right hemispheres and promotes clear thinking.
- Benefits in following conditions-asthma, allergies, high or low blood pressure, stress-related heart conditions, hyperactivity, insomnia, chronic pain, endocrine imbalances and psychological conditions as anxiety, stress, etc.

Contraindications

- Keep the ratio of 1:1 between inhalation and exhalation.
- Avoid producing any sound from the nose.
- Avoid pressing hard on the nostrils.

Hypertension

Hypertension is also known as high blood pressure. In hypertension, the blood pressure of body goes beyond 140/90 mm/Hg. The normal body pressure of an adult person is considered as 120/80 mm/Hg.

The situation of hypertension arises when heart pumps more blood than normal situation and arteries become narrower.

Earlier, it was considered as a middle-age problem but now-a-days, youngsters also suffer from this problem due to their faulty lifestyle. Hypertension is a primary risk factor for cardiovascular disease, including stroke, heart attack, heart failure and aneurysm.

Note *Tadasana, Katichakrasana, Gomukhasana, Uttana Mandukasana, Vakrasana, Bhujangasana and Sitali Pranayama are already discussed previously in the chapter.*

Uttana Padasana

Procedure

- Lie on the floor, facing the ceiling.
- Keep legs stretched, feet close to each other, tightly at the arches, toes facing upwards towards the ceiling.
- Keep upper limbs by the side of your body, close to it, palms down.
- Inhale
- Lift both legs in air as you inhale. While doing this keep the torso on the floor. Allow the lower back to arch slightly.
- Tuck your chin towards neck. Squeeze the thighs together and tuck your stomach in. Reach out with your toes such that the toes point the ceiling.
- The legs are approximately at an angle of 30 degrees from the floor. This is good at beginner level. If you get comfortable in the pose gradually and when you feel your body is flexible enough you can extend the angle to 45 or even 60 degrees.
- Be there for 4-5 breaths or for 30 seconds to 2 minutes or as you feel comfortable doing it. Repeat it for 8-10 times.

Benefits

- It opens up the chest, contracts the abdomen and stretches the arms and legs simultaneously.
- It increases flexibility of internal and external muscles.
- It relieves stiffness in the lower back, back ache, pain in hips and joints.
- It strengthens abdominal muscles, nerves, spinal cord and reproductive system.
- It enhances blood circulation to heart and neck.
- It cures digestive and intestinal disorders.

Contraindications

- It should be avoided by persons suffering from high blood pressure, back, hip, knee or leg injury and abdominal surgery.
- It should be avoided by women during pregnancy and menstruation.

Ardha Halasana

Procedure

- Lie down in Shavasana (supine position).
- Join the both legs and keep your hand with the thighs.
- Slowly breathe in and raise the leg perpendicular to the ground keeping the knee straight.
- Hold in the breathe and stay in this position as long as possible.
- Breathe out and bring back your legs.
- Come back to the normal position and relax for a while.
- Repeat the same for 3 to 5 times.
- The above mentioned technique can also be performed only with a single one after the other.

Benefits

- It improves digestion and appetite.
- It improve blood circulation.
- It strengthens the thigh muscles and calf muscles.
- It is helpful to reduce abdomen fat and lose weight.
- It stimulates the abdominal organs.

Contraindications

It should be avoided by people suffering from any cardiac problem, back pain, high blood pressure.

Sarala Matsyasana

Procedure

- Lay flat on the back.
- With the support of your hands keep the top of your head on the mat.
- Neck, upper back and shoulders will be lifted from the ground.
- Relax your hands at the side of your body.
- Breathe normally and keep your toes stretched out.
- Hold the position for 30 seconds and relax.

Benefits

- It improves the digestion system.
- It helps to cure irritable bowel syndrome.
- It helps to get rid of abdominal-related issues.

Contraindications

It should be avoided by persons with cervical spondylitis and frozen shoulder.

Makrasana

Procedure

- Lie down straight on your stomach.
- Now join your elbows, making a stand and place your palms under the chin.
- Lift your chest up.
- Keep your elbows and legs together.
- During inhaling, first, fold your one leg at a time and then both the legs together.
- During folding, your ankles should touch the hips.
- While exhaling, your feet should be straight and keep your head steady.
- Repeat this for 20 to 25 times.

Benefits

- It is beneficial in cervical, slip disc, spondylitis, sciatica.

- It is beneficial in all spine related problems.
- It stretches the muscles of legs and hips.
- It is best for relaxing after doing other asanas.

Contraindications

- It should be avoided by persons suffering from back injury, neck injury and psychological issues.
- It should be avoided by women during pregnancy.

Shavasana (Corpse Pose)

Procedure

- This is done in lying position.
- Lie flat on the back, like in sleeping pose and separate the legs.
- Keep the arms at side and palms facing up and relax.
- Close the eyes and breathe deeply and slowly through the nostrils.
- Start concentrating from the head to feet. Feel relaxation in each part of the body.
- On each inhaling and exhaling (breathing), body should be relaxed.
- Stay in this pose for 10 to 15 minutes.

Benefits

- It relaxes the whole body.
- It releases stress, fatigue, depression and tension.
- It improves concentration and cures insomnia.
- It helps to calm the mind and improves mental health.
- It regulates blood circulation.
- It gives new vigour to both mind and body simultaneously.

Contraindication

Usually, there is no contraindication of this asana, except where the doctor has advised not to lie on back.

Sitali Pranayama

Procedure

- Sit in front of yoga mat at any meditative posture like Padmasana, Sukhasana or in Vajrasana with head, neck, and spine erect in one line. Also, to make practice more effective, you can make Gyan Mudra with your hands.
- Breathe in deeply 2-3 times with your mouth open, and exhale from the nose to prepare for the sitali breathing.
- Bring out your tongue while curling it on sides towards the center to form a tube-like shape.
- Now inhale through the tube-form tongue and towards the end of inhalation, lower your chin to the chest in 'Jalandhara Bandha'. At this point, hold your breath for 6-8 secs.
- Before exhaling, lift up your chin, withdraw your tongue & close your mouth. Now exhale completely through your nostrils. This completes one round sitali breathing.

Benefits

- It relieves stress and anxiety through its soothing and relaxing effect.
- It also helps reduce fever by bringing down body temperature.
- It helps calm down hunger and thirst in an emergency situation.
- It also helps in lowering blood pressure.
- It is very useful for people suffering from insomnia.
- It is very helpful for people suffering from a sleep disorder.

Contraindications

- Sitali Pranayama should be avoided by persons with low blood pressure, respiratory disorders and chronic constipation.

Nadi Shodhana Pranayama

Procedure

- This is done in a sitting position.
- Bring the right hand into Vishnu Mudra (thumb to the right nostril, ring and pinky fingers to left, index and middle finger folded and resting at the base of the thumb).
- Exhale completely.
- Block the right nostril and inhale through left nostril.
- Release right nostril and exhale.
- Block left nostril and inhale right.
- Release left nostril and exhale.
- This completes 1 full cycle and repeat 10 to 12 cycler.

Benefits

- It helps to calm and steadies the mind, improves focus and concentration.
- Stimulates calming centres of the brain.
- Opens the nadis (energy channels), removes blockages from them and facilitates flow of energy throughout the body.
- Improves blood supply to brain.

Contraindications

- Avoid practicing of this pranayam in the condition of cold or running nose.
- Patients with sinus should avoid practicing.
- Avoid practicing of this pranayama around the dirty place.

Previous Years'

Examination & Other Important Questions

☑ 1 Mark Questions (MCQ)

1. Which one of the following asanas is not a remedial asana for treating obesity?
(a) Vajrasana
(b) Tadasana
(c) Halasana
(d) Ardha-Matsyendrasana

Ans. (a) Vajrasana

2. Which of the following is a medical condition which causes lifestyle diseases?
(a) Diabete
(b) Hypertension
(c) Asthma
(d) Obesity

Ans. (d) Obesity

3. Which of the following asanas is beneficial in reducing obesity?
(a) Matsyasana (b) Gomukhasana
(c) Kapalabhati (d) None of these

Ans. (a) Matsyasana

4. Which of the following asanas is beneficial in the lifestyle diseases of diabetes, asthma and hypertension ?
(a) Pavan Muktasana
(b) Tadasana
(c) Bhujangasana
(d) Trikonasana

Ans. (c) Bhujangasana

5. Asthma can be reduced by performing .... and ....
(a) Sukhasana, Trikonasana
(b) Chakrasana, Tadasana
(c) Ardh Matsyendrasana, Matsyasana
(d) None of the above

Ans. (d) None of the above

6. Which of the following is not a benefit of Hastasana?
(a) It helps in shoulder and neck injuries.
(b) It stretches the entire body.
(c) It stretches the organs of the abdomen.
(d) It enhances blood circulation.

Ans. (a) It helps in shoulder and neck injuries.

7. .... is done in a sitting posture.
(a) Bhujangasana
(b) Pavan muktasana
(c) Trikonasana
(d) Gomukhasana

Ans. (d) Gomukhasana

8. Which of the following asanas is also called as 'Mountain pose'?
(a) Vajrasana
(b) Tadasana
(c) Gomukhasana
(d) Trikonasana

Ans. (b) Tadasana

9. Out of the following asanas, which one is contraindicated if suffering high blood pressure or heart problems?
(a) Sukhasana
(b) Gomukhasana
(c) Pavan Muktasana
(d) All of the above

Ans. (c) Pavan Muktasana

10. Which one of the following asanas is most beneficial for improving body posture?
(a) Tadasana
(b) Gomukhasana
(c) Shavasana
(d) None of the above

Ans. (a) Tadasana

11. Which of the following is a contraindication for Shavasana?
(a) High blood pressure
(b) Obesity
(c) Liver enlargement
(d) None of the above

Ans. (d) None of the above

12. Which of the following are benefits of performing Vakrasana?
(a) It helps in healing of ulcers and hernia.
(b) It helps in controlling waist pain and chronic back pain.
(c) Both (a) and (b)
(d) Neither (a) nor (b)

Ans. *(b)* It helps in controlling waist pain and chronic back pain.

13. Shalabhasana is beneficial for ....
(a) removing unwanted fat around waist, hips and thighs
(b) back pain
(c) Both (a) and (b)
(d) Neither (a) nor (b)

Ans. *(c)* Both (a) and (b)

14. Paschimottasana is contraindicated in case of ....
(a) migraine (b) low blood pressure
(c) pregnancy (d) All of these

Ans. *(c)* pregnancy

🗗 1 Mark Questions [VSA]

1. Define yoga.

Ans. Yoga is an ancient science that harmonises the body, mind and spirit.

2. What is hypertension? **CBSE 2018**

Ans. Hypertension, also known as high blood pressure, is a long-term medical condition in which the blood pressure in the arteries is continually elevated.

3. Name any one asana to cure obesity.

Ans. Tadasana is an asana that cures obesity.

4. Explain the contraindication of Hastasna.

Ans. In case of shoulder or neck injuries, experiencing dizziness while staring upwards and in case of any other medical concerns.

5. Discuss the two contraindications of Trikonasana.

Ans. *Two contraindications of Trikonasana are as follows*
(*i*) Avoid doing this if suffering from migraine, diarrhoea, low or high blood pressure.
(*ii*) Avoid if having a problem of neck and back injuries.

6. What do you understand by the Ardha Matsyendrasana?

Ans. Ardha Matsyendrasana or the half spinal twist pose is one the main asanas practised in hatha yoga. This yoga helps in stimulating the liver. It is also therapeutic for asthma and infertility etc.

7. Discuss any two benefits of Paschimottasana.

Ans. *Two benefits of Paschimottasana are as follows*
(*i*) It helps to remove constipation and digestive disorder.
(*ii*) It reduces headache, anxiety and insomnia.

8. Write any two benefits of Pawanmuktasana.

Ans. *Two benefits of Pawanmuktasana are as follows*
(*i*) It helps to strengthen the back muscles and cure backpain.
(*ii*) It cures acidity, indigestion and constipation.

9. Write any two benefits of the Gomukhasana.

Ans. *The two benefits of Gomukhasana are as follows*
(*i*) It is helpful in the treatment of sciatica.
(*ii*) It enhances the workings of the kidneys by stimulating it, thus helping those suffering from diabetes.

10. State two contraindication of Tadasana.

Ans. *The two contraindications of Tadasana are as follows*
(*i*) Avoid during insomnia.
(*ii*) Avoid during low blood pressure.

🗗 3 Marks Questions

1. Explain about the procedure and advantages of Bhujangasana in the context of diabetes. **CBSE 2019**

Ans. There are many procedure as well as advantages of Bhujangasana.

Procedure
The procedure of Bhujangasana is as follows
- This is done in lying posture.
- Lie on the stomach and rest forehead on the floor.
- Keep the feet and toes together and touch the ground. Place the hands at shoulder level and palms on floor.
- Inhale and lift the head, chest abdomen. Keep the navel on the floor and take at least five breaths.
- Exhale slowly and come to rest with hands below the head.

Advantages

The advantages of practising Bhujangasana regularly in the context of diabetes are as follows

- It improves the blood circulation and energises the heart.
- It decreases menstrual irregularities in females.
- It strengthens muscles of chest, shoulders, arms and abdomen.
- It is effective in uterine disorders.
- It improves the function of reproductive organs.
- It improves the function of liver, kidney, pancreas and gall bladder.
- It helps to lose weight.

2. Explain the procedure of Pawanmuktasana.

Ans. There are following ways to do this asana

- This is done in lying position.
- Lie flat on the back and keep the legs straight, relax, breathe deeply and regularly.
- Inhale slowly and lift the legs and bend in the knees. Bring upwards to the chest till the thigh touches to stomach.
- Hug the knees in place and lock the fingers.
- Place the nose tip between the knees.
- Exhale slowly and come back to the original position i.e. Shavasana.
- This is very beneficial for stomach abs. The results are very impressive.

3. Explain the procedures of Paschimottasana.

Ans. There are following ways to do this asana

- This is done in sitting posture.
- Sit on the floor with the outstretched legs.
- Inhale and lengthen the abdomen then lift the chest.
- Exhale, bend forwards from the hips. Keep the shoulders open and the head up.
- Reach forwards and hold the big toes in a lock with the middle and index fingers.
- Inhale, lengthen the torso, bring the sternum forward.
- Exhale, bring the chest and abdomen down to the thighs and the elbows out to the sides.
- Stay in this position for 5 deep breaths and relax the muscles while exhale.
- Focus on stretching the hamstrings rather than getting the head to the knees.

4. Write the detail about the benefits of Hastasana.

Ans. There are some benefits of Hastasana as follows

- It stretches the complete body and provides a good massage to the arms, spine, upper and lower back, ankles, hands, shoulders, calf muscles and thighs.
- It stretches the organs of the stomach and as a result enhances the digestive system and increases the capacity of the lungs.
- This asana helps in enhancing the blood circulation of the body.
- It helps in enhancing the body postures.
- It helps in alleviating nervousness and melancholy along with providing a sense of achievement.
- It helps in tightening the abdomen and helps in easing sciatica.

5. State the contraindication of Gomukhasana and Bhujangasana.

Ans. There are following contraindications of Gomukhasana

- Those who are suffering from shoulder, knee or back pain should avoid this.
- Suffering from any kind of knee injury/problem avoid this.
- There are following contraindications of Bhujangasana
- Avoid during pregnancy.
- People having a hernia problem and back ache should not do this asana.
- Avoid those who are suffering from ulcer, heart problem or any surgeries like spine and brain.

6. Explain the benefits and contraindications of Vakrasana.

Ans. **Benefits**

There are following benefits of Vakrasana

- It reduces belly fat.
- It improves the function of both spinal cord and nervous system.
- It controls diabetes and strengthens kidneys.
- It kindles adrenal gland to function properly.
- It helps to control waist, back pain and chronic backpain.

Contraindications

- Avoid if suffering from ulcer and enlargement of liver.
- Avoid suffering from severe backpain, ulcer and hernia.

7. Neeti along with her father was regular at District Park in early morning. She realized that most of the children are obese. She along with her few classmates wanted to help those children. She discussed with her physical education teacher and the Principal of the school. School decided to organize awareness rally for the neighbourhood. **CBSE QB 2021**

(i) Obesity causes
   (a) Underweight (b) Diabetes
   (c) Back pain   (d) Both (b) and (c)

(ii) Which of the following Asana (posture) is used for curing obesity?
   (a) Ardhmatsyendrasana
   (b) Vajrasana
   (c) Parvatasana
   (d) Trikonasana

(iii) Choose the Asana which is not used for curing obesity.
   (a) Sukhasana   (b) Shavasana
   (c) Vajrasana   (d) All of these

Ans. (i) - (c),   (ii) - (a),   (iii) - (d)

8. Raman is a student of class VIII and is suffering from Obesity. During a recent medical checkup at school, he was advised to practice yoga and participate in sports activities for curing it. He consulted the yoga instructor at the school for further guidance.

Based on this case answer the following questions: **CBSE QB 2021**

(i) The yoga instructor at the school has asked Raman to perform
   (a) Bhujangasana   (b) Pawanmuktasana
   (c) Vajrasana   (d) Chakrasana

(ii) The BMI index for an Obese person is
   (a) <18.5   (b) 18.5-24.9
   (c) >30   (d) >25

(iii) Due to the Obesity; Raman is also suffering from knock knees for which he is advised to
   (a) Walk on inner edge of foot
   (b) Walk on outer edge of foot
   (c) Walk on heels   (d) Walk on toes

Ans. (i) - (b),   (ii) - (c),   (iii) - (b)

9. Shruti, a yoga instructor at XYZ students. She was able to make a pie chart on the basis of the data. On the basis of the chart answer the following questions.
CBSE QB 2021

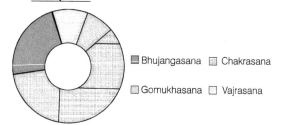

(i) Which is the most famous asana?
   (a) Bhujangasana
   (b) Chakrasana
   (c) Gomukhasana
   (d) Vajrasana

(ii) Which amongst these is a lying asana?
   (a) Vajrasana   (b) Bhujangasana
   (c) Chakrasana   (d) Gomukhasana

(iii) Which amongst these is used to prevent Diabetes?
   (a) Bhujangasana   (b) Tadasana
   (c) Chakrasana   (d) Vajrasana

Ans. (i) - (b),   (ii) - (a),   (iii) - (a)

10. Gunjan, a Yoga instructor at XYZ School was consulted by a student of class XI in relation to her over weight. The child wants to do asanas to reduce her weight.
CBSE QB 2021

(i) Gunjan has asked the child to practice ....
   (a) Paschimottanasana
   (b) Gomukhasana
   (c) Chakrasana
   (d) Vajrasana

(ii) While practicing this asana child should not be suffering from ....
   (a) Joint pain   (b) High BP
   (c) Scurvy   (d) Constipation

(iii) This asana is .... asana.
   (a) Standing   (b) Relaxative
   (c) Meditative   (d) Lying

Ans. (i) - (c),   (ii) - (a),   (iii) - (d)

📱 5 Marks Questions

1. Write the benefits and contraindications of Matsyasana. **CBSE Term II 2022**

Ans. **Benefits**
  - It stretches the neck muscles and shoulders.
  - This pose provides relief from respiratory disorders by encouraging deep breathing, as this pose increases lung capacity to a great extent.
  - There is an increased supply of blood to the cervical and thoracic regions of the back that helps tone the parathyroid, pituitary and pineal glands.
  - This pose helps to regulate emotions and stress.
  - The practice of Matsyasana brings down the tension and the stiffness at the neck and the shoulders.

  Contraindications
  - Individuals suffering from high or low blood pressure should avoid this posture.
  - Women who are pregnant should not attempt this yoga pose.
  - Injury in neck or any part of the lower back or middle back can make it difficult to practice this fish pose and hence should be avoided.

2. What is obesity? Draw stick diagrams of any two asanas recommended of control obesity and explain their procedure. **CBSE Term II 2022**

Ans. Obesity is referred to as a medical condition in which excess body fat is accumulated to that extent that it has a negative effect on health. Obesity in itself is not a disease but the condition of obesity leads to many diseases. This is because a person becomes extremely fat and the glands and other body system cannot function properly. When the body does not function properly then it gives rise to many cardiovascular diseases, etc.

  Pavanamuktasana

  Procedure
  - This is done in lying position.
  - Lie flat on the back, keep the legs straight and relax your body.
  - Inhale slowly and lift the legs and bend on the knees. Bring upwards to the chest till the thigh touches the stomach.
  - Hug the knees and lock the fingers.
  - Place the nose tip between the knees.
  - Exhale slowly and come back to the original position.

  Tadasana (Mountain Pose)

  Procedure
  - This is done in standing position.
  - Stand straight and join the feet together.
  - Toes must touch each other and heels may be slightly apart.
  - With deep inhalation, raise up both the arms and then interlock the fingers.
  - Stretch your shoulders and chest upward.
  - Hold for 4 to 8 breaths.
  - Exhale and drop the shoulders down.

3. Explain the procedure and benefits of any one asana used to cure diabetes.**CBSE 2020**

Ans. For procedure of Pavanmuktasana, refer to Q. No. 2 (5 Marks Questions) on page no 39.

Benefits of Pavanamuktasana are

- It cures acidity, indigestion and constipation.
- It is helpful for those suffering from gastrointestinal problems, arthritis, heart problems and waist and back pain.
- This is very beneficial for stomach abs. The results are very impressive.
- It strengthens back muscle and cures back pain.

It is very beneficial for reproductive organs and for menstruation disorder.

4. Explain about the procedure and advantages of 'Bhujangasana'. **CBSE 2019**

Ans. Refer to Q. No. 1 (3 Marks Questions) on page no 36 and 37.

5. Briefly explain the symptoms and causes of Asthma. Explain the procedure, benefits and contraindications of any two asanas to prevent Asthma. **CBSE 2018**

Ans. Asthma is a condition in which a person's airways in the lungs are inflamed and narrowed, making it difficult for the air to move in and out, thus causing difficulty in breathing. It is a chronic disease and lasts lifelong.

Causes of Asthma

- Allergy for airborne substances such as pollen grains, dust, mites, molds, spores etc.
- Air pollutants and irritants such as smoke suspended in the air.
- Respiratory infections such as common cold.

Symptoms of Asthma

- Shortness of breath
- Coughing/ sneezing too much
- Frequent respiratory infections
- Fast heart rate

Asanas for Asthma

Asanas that can cure or help to manage asthma are Urdhvahastasana, Uttanamandukasana Tadasana etc.

Urdhva Hastasana

Procedure

- Stand in a Tadasana (Mountain pose). Then, gently raise your hand upward.
- Bring the arms parallel to one another and then without bending the shoulders, bring your arms together over your head.
- Expand the elbows completely and reach upwards. Then slightly slant your head backwards and look at the thumbs.
- Shoulder blades must be pressed firmly on your back.
- Bring your buttock inward by compressing them.
- Keep your feet together and press your heel firmly against the ground.

Benefits

- It stretches the complete body and provides a good massage to the arms, spine, upper and lower back, ankles, hands, shoulders, calf muscles and thighs.
- It enhances the functioning of digestive system and increases the capacity of the lungs.

Contraindications

- Avoid in case of shoulder or neck injuries.
- Avoid if experiencing dizziness while staring upwards and in case of any other medical concerns.

Uttana Mandukasana

Procedure

- Sit in Vajrasana.
- Spread both the knees wide apart while toes remaining together.
- Raise your right arm, fold it and take it backward from above the right shoulder and place the palm below the left shoulder.
- Now fold the left arm similarly and place the palm from above below the right shoulder.
- Maintain the position. While coming back, slowly remove the left arm and then right arm; bring the knees together as in the initial position.

Benefits

- It gives stretch to the throat muscles and nerves and relieves throat pain.
- It gives good stretch to the upper and lower back muscles, makes back muscles flexible and relieves back pain and strain.

Contraindications

- It should be avoided by persons suffering from arthritis, hernia, chronic and severe back problems, knee problems, elbow pain and severe shoulder pain, spinal cord deformities and disabilities of hip joints.

6. Elaborate the benefits of Tadasana and Shalabhasana.

Ans. There are various benefits of these asanas

Benefits of Tadasana

- It improves body posture and reduces flat feet problem.
- Knees, thighs and ankles become stronger.
- Buttocks and abdomen get toned.
- It helps to alleviate sciatica.
- It makes spine more agile.
- It helps to increase height and improve balance.
- It regulates digestive, nervous and respiratory systems.

Benefits of Shalabhasana

- It is beneficial in problems of the spine.
- It is helpful for backache and sciatica pain.
- It is helpful to remove unwanted fat around abdomen, waist, hips and thighs.
- It can cure cervical spondylitis and spinal cord ailments.
- It gives flexibility to the back muscles and spine.
- It can strengthen the shoulder and neck muscles.

7. Explain the contraindications of Trikonasana, Ardha Matsyendrasana and Bhujangasana.

Ans. Contraindications of Trikonasana

- Avoid doing this if suffering from migraine, diarrhoea, neck and back injuries.
- Those with high blood pressure may do this pose but without raising their hand overhead, as this may further raise the blood pressure.

Contraindications of Ardha Matsyendrasana

- Avoid during pregnancy and menstruation due to the strong twist in the abdomen.
- People with heart, abdominal or brain surgeries should avoid this asana.
- Those who are having peptic ulcer or hernia should avoid it.
- Those with severe spinal problems should avoid it.
- Those with mild slipped disc can benefit, but in severe cases it should be avoided.

Contraindications of Bhujangasana

- Avoid during pregnancy.
- People having a hernia problem and backache should not do this asana.
- Those who are suffering from ulcer, heart problem or any surgeries of the spine and brain should avoid it.

8. What are the procedure of Tadasana, Pawanmuktasana and Ardha Chakrasana?

Ans. For procedure of Tadasana and Pawanmuktasana, refer to Q.No. 2 (5 Marks Questions) on page no. 39.

Procedure of Ardha Chakrasana

- This is a standing asana.
- Stand straight with arms alongside the body.
- Balance the weight equally on both feet.
- Breathing in, extend the arms overhead with palms facing each other.
- Bend backwards, push the pelvis forward, keep the arms in line with the ears, elbows and knees straight, head up, and lift the chest towards the ceiling.
- Breathe out, bring the arms down and relax.

9. Elucidate the benefits and contraindication of Vakrasana and Vajrasana.

Ans. Benefits of Vakrasana

For the benefits and contraindication of Vakrasana, refer to Q. No. 6 (3 Marks Questions) on page no. 37.

Benefits of Vajrasana

- It enhances blood circulation.
- It helps to improve digestion.
- Food gets digested well if one sits in Vajrasana after taking meals.
- It relieves excessive gas trouble or pain.
- Nerves of legs and thighs are strengthened.
- It helps to make knee and ankle joints flexible.
- It prevents certain rheumatic diseases.

Contraindications of Vajrasana
- Avoid if there is acute trouble or stiffness in foot, ankle and knees.
- Avoid during slipped disc conditions.

10. Briefly explain the administration of Pawanmuktasana along with its contraindications.

Ans. The administration of Pawanmuktasana is
- Lie on your back with your feet together and arms besides your body and relax, breathing deeply.
- With a deep inhalation raise your legs to 90° and completely exhale.
- Now with another inhalation bring both the knees close to your chest and press on the lower abdomen, holding the knees with your hands. Exhale completely.
- Remain with bent knees for a few breaths. With every exhalation press the thighs and knees on the abdomen and hold them with your hands.
- With a deep breath raise your head, neck and chest and bring them close to your knees.
- Remain in this posture for a few breaths focusing on maintaining the position of the head and neck in place.
- Try to maintain the balance while breathing slowly and keeping the body relaxed.
- Now with an inhalation, release the neck and head and exhale completely. With another inhalation straighten the legs and bring them back to 90° and as you exhale release the leg from 90° to the relaxed posture. With complete exhalation, bring the legs stretched out on the floor and relax the neck.
- Take a few breaths, and then continue with the next round. The longer you hold in this posture the faster the muscles around the abdomen loosen.

Contraindications of Pawanmuktasana is that it is to be avoided by those who are suffering from severe migraine, high or low blood pressure, asthma, slip disc, advanced stages of spondylitis, etc.

11.

(i) The above pose can be identified as
CBSE QB 2021
(a) Vajrasana
(b) Trikonasana
(c) Chakrasana
(d) Padmasana

(ii) This asana is used to cure
(a) Obesity
(b) diabetes
(c) Knee pain
(d) Asthma

(iii) Normal Blood pressure is an adult is
....
(a) 120/80mm
(b) 140/90mm
(c) 80/100mm
(d) 100/80mm

(iv) This asana is contraindicated when a person is suffering with ....
(a) knee pains
(b) gastric problem
(c) sciatica
(d) hernia

(v) While performing this asana, breathing should be ....
(a) slower
(b) faster
(c) only inhale
(d) only exhale

Ans. (i) - (a),   (ii) - (b),   (iii) - (a),   (iv) - (a),   (v) - (a)

12. Mr. Shyam aged 50 years is recommended to practice the below asana as a therapeutic measure. He is a software engineer by occupation and spends lot of time sitting at one place. He developed certain symptoms like frequent urge for urination, tiredness, excessive weight gain along with being anxious and gets easily irritated.

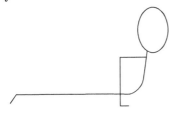

(i) From the shape of the body in the given pose, it can identified as ......
   (a) Gomukhasan   (b) Bhujangasan
   (c) Tadasan   (d) Vajrasan

(ii) Mr.Shyam is diagnosed with ....
   (a) Diabetes
   (b) Both Diabetes and Hypertension
   (b) hypertension
   (d) Obesity

(iii) Blood sugar levels are controlled by .... hormone.
   (a) Thyroxin
   (b) Insulin
   (c) Pituitary
   (d) Progesterone

(iv) This asana should be avoided by people suffering with ....
   (a) Obesity   (b) Hernia
   (c) Diabetes   (d) Hypertension

(v) The disease of lung where airways are blocked or narrowed is ....
   (a) Diabetes   (b) Asthma
   (c) Obesity   (d) Hypertension

Ans. (i) - (b),   (ii) - (b),   (iii) - (b),   (iv) - (b),   (v) - (b)

CHAPTER 04

Physical Education & Sports for CWSN

Organisations Promoting Disability/Adaptive Sports

For the promotion and organisation of adaptive sports, many different competitions are held. Some of them are **Special Olympics, Paralympics, Deaflympics** etc. These competitions provide a good platform for individuals with disabilities to participate.

Special Olympics

The idea of Special Olymipcs initiated by Eunice Mary Kennedy Shriver. She believed that with equal opportunities and experience as everyone else, people with intellectual disabilities could compete far more than ever thought possible. The first Special Olympic games were held in Chicago in July, 1968.

The US Olympics Committee gave the Special Olympics an official approval to use the name 'Olympics' in 1971. The United Nations declared 1986 as the year of Special Olympics. The Special Olympics were officially organised in 1988 by International Olympics Committee.

Special Olympics Logo

The logo of Special Olympics is based on the Sculpture 'Joy and Happiness to all Children of the World'.

Years and Venues of Special Olympics

S.No.	Year	City	Country
I	1968	Chicago	USA
II	1970	Chicago	USA
III	1972	Los Angeles	USA
IV	1975	Mount Pleasant	USA

S.No.	Year	City	Country
V	1979	Brokport	USA
VI	1983	Baton Rouge	USA
VII	1987	Notre Dame and South Bend	USA
VIII	1991	Minneapolis and Saint Paul	USA
IX	1995	New Haven	USA
X	1999	CH Durham and Raleigh	USA
XI	2003	Dublin	Ireland
XII	2007	Shanghai	China
XIII	2011	Athens	Greece
XIV	2015	Los Angeles	USA
XV	2019	Abu Dhabi	UAE
XVI	2023	Berlin (Scheduled)	Germany

Sports and Games in Special Olympics

In Special Olympics, the games and sports included are

- Skiing : Alpine and Cross-country
- Swimming : Pool and Open Water
- Gymnastics : Artistic and Rhythmic
- Speed Skating; Short Track
- Handball
- Netball
- Equestrian
- Athletics (Track and Field)
- Softball
- Judo
- Figure Skating
- Powerlifting
- Basketball
- Floor Hockey
- Table Tennis
- Football (Soccer)
- Tennis
- Golf
- Triathlon
- Cycling
- Snowshoe, Running
- Badminton
- Floorball
- Kayaking
- Bocce
- Roller Skating
- Bowling
- Sailing
- Cricket
- Snowboarding
- Volleyball

Paralympics

The Paralympic games are major international multi-sports event involving athletes with various disabilities such as impaired muscle power, impaired passive range of movement, limb deficiency, leg-length difference short stature, hypertonia, ataxia, athetosis, visual and intellectual impairment, blindness, etc.

The originator of the Paralympic Games is **Sir Ludwig Guttmann**. The first Paralympic games were organised in Rome in 1960. The word Paralympic was officially used in 1988.

The word Paralympic is derived from the Greek Preposition 'Para' means besides or alongside and the word 'Olympic'. It signifies that Paralympics are the parallel games to the Olympics.

International Paralympic Committee (IPC)

The International Paralympic Committee is the global governing body of the Paralympic movement. Its purpose is to organise the Summer and Winter Paralympic Games. It was formed on 22nd September, 1989 in Dusseldorf. Its headquarter is located in Bonn, Germany.

The aim of IPC is to promote paralympic values and to create sport opportunities for all persons with a disability, from beginner to elite level.

Paralympic Motto

The Paralympic motto is 'Spirit in Motion'. The motto was introduced in 2004 at the Paralympic Games, Athenes. It's earlier motto was 'Mind, Body and Spirit', which was introduced in 1994.

Minimum Disability Criteria Each sport's Paralympic classification rules describe how severe an eligible impairment must be for an athlete to be considered eligible. These criteria are referred to as minimum disability criteria.

Opening Ceremony

The opening ceremony of the Paralympic Games starts with the hoisting of the host country's flag and rendition of its national anthem. Thereafter, the athletes come for march past into the stadium grouped according to their country. All the countries enter the stadium alphabetically according to the host country's chosen language. But, the athletes of the host country enter last into the stadium.

Awards

The medals are presented to the winners as awards after every Paralympic event. The competitors or teams that secure first, second and third position stand-up at the victory podium and are awarded with the medals.

Then, the tune of the national song of the gold medalist's country is played and the national flags of three countries are unfurled and hoisted.

Closing Ceremony

The closing ceremony begin after all sport events finishes. Flag bearers from each participating country enter the stadium followed by athletes who enter together without any national distinction. The Paralympic flag is taken down. The games are officially closed and the paralympics flame is extinguished.

Paralympic Sports

The Summer Paralympics consists of 22 sports, while the Winter Paralympics consists of 6.

The list of Summer Paralympics (Sports) are as follows

- Athletics
- Bocce
- Archery
- Wheelchair Tennis
- Shooting
- Equestrian
- Wheelchair Rugby
- Football 5-a-side
- Goalball
- Table Tennis
- Wheelchair Basketball
- Para Triathlon
- Para Taekwondo
- Rowing
- Cycling
- Sitting Volleyball
- Powerlifting
- Swimming
- Wheelchair Fencing
- Para Canoe
- Judo
- Para Badminton

Paralympic Games Logo

Deaflympics

Deaflympics is an international Olympic event at which deaf athletes compete. Unlike other paralympic events, deaf athletes cannot be guided by sounds like referee whistle, gunshot etc. Therefore, special arrangements are made for the deaf athletes at Deaflympics such as waving a flag, using light instead of gunshots etc.

The Deaflympics are more than just the world's second oldest multiple sports after olympics. These games are the world's fastest growing sports events.

The Deaflympics are an equivalent to the Olympic games for deaf athletes. These games have been organised by the International Committee of sports for deaf since the first event.

The first of such games were held in Paris in 1924. Since then, these games have been held regularly after every four years. The Deaflympics Winter Games were started in 1949.

DEAFLYMPICS

Deaflympics Logo

The Motto of Deaflympics is *'Per Ludos Aequalitas'* meaning *'Equality through sports'*. It's logo is inspired by the sign for Olympics. The circle in the middle represents an eye because deaf people are very visual.

The four colours of the logo *i.e.* red, green, yellow and blue represent the four regional confederations of the International Committee of Sports for Deaf *viz.* Europe, Asia Pacific, Pan-America and Africa.

Year and Venue of Winter Deaflympics

S. No.	Year	City	Country
I	1949	Seefeld	Austria
II	1953	Oslo	Norway
III	1955	Oberammergaau	Germany
IV	1959	Montana-Vennala	Switzerland
V	1963	Are	Sweden
VI	1967	Berchtesgaden	West Germany
VII	1971	Adelboden	Switzerland
VIII	1975	Lake Placid	United States
IX	1979	Meribel	France
X	1983	Madonna di Campiglio	Italy
XI	1987	Oslo	Norway
XII	1991	Banff	Canada
XIII	1995	Yllas	Finland
XIV	1999	Davos	Switzerland
XV	2003	Sundsvall	Sweden
XVI	2007	Salt Lake City	United States
XVII	2011	Vysoke Tatry, Slovakia	Slovakia
XVIII	2015	Khanty-Mansiyak	Russia
XIX	2019	Sondrio Province	Italy
XX	2023	Quebec City	Canada

Advantage of Physical Activity for Children With Special Needs

Physical Activity

According to the Department of Health and Human Services, USA, physical activity generally refers to movement that enhances health.

It means the movement of the body that uses energy. Walking, running, dancing, swimming, yoga and gardening are a few examples of physical activity. For health benefits, physical activity should be of moderate or vigorous intensity.

Exercise is a type of physical activity that's planned and structured. Lifting weights, participating in an aerobics class and playing on a sports team are examples of exercise.

Advantage of Physical Activity for Children with Special Needs

Regular physical activity is good for everyone but it's particularly important for children with special needs. It is most important for their growth and development. There are a number of advantages of physical activities for such persons.

These are as follows

- It strengthens the heart muscle, thereby improving cardiovascular efficiency, lung efficiency and exercise endurance. This helps in controlling repetitive behaviour among disabled children.
- Besides improving fitness, physical activity develops social relationships with other children, teammates and teachers. This brings positive changes in the social behaviour of these children.
- It helps to improve energy level in the body. Regular physical activity often makes children more energetic and allows them to become active.
- It regulates blood pressure, cholesterol level and diabetes. Physical activity also reduces stress level.
- It helps to control weight. Children with disabilities are normally not physically active or may have a deficit of calories, which takes fat away and lowers weight. Regular exercises help in regulating weight.
- Physical activities help in improving muscle strength, coordination and flexibility among disabled children.
- It also improves motor skills, brings better balance and body awareness which is lacking in these children.
- Physical exercise finds an outlet to channelise the physical energy which helps these children to cope with stress, anxiety and depression.

- Physical activity enhances the metabolism of brain in the children. It leads to cognitive improvement in children with special needs, allowing them to acquire new skills, learn new things and focus on specific goals.
- Physical activity decreases anxiety, reduces depression, and improves mood and outlook in children. In addition, their quality of sleep is improved.

Strategies to Make Physical Activities Accessible for Children with Special Needs

The various strategies or ways by which physical activities can be made accessible to children with special needs are as follows

(*i*) **Inclusive Classrooms** It means development of educational laws in such a way that children with special needs get education within the normal classrooms along with other children so that they are well accepted in society.

(*ii*) **Assistive Technology** It refers to creating devices, tools or equipment that help children with special needs to participate in learning activities such as bigger balls, balls with bells, balls attached to strings to bring it back to the students, etc.

(*iii*) **Adaptive Physical Education** Depending on student's disability, a separate, adaptive class or modifications within a game, or changing the rules of the game or sport to some extent, can help the students in a big way.

(*iv*) **Creating Specific Environment** Students with special needs can be provided with specific play area with special requirements as needed by them. Loud music, glaring lights often cannot be tolerated by these children, so a lot of natural lighting should be there.

(*v*) **Positive Behaviour** In physical education classes, teachers should show positive behaviour and healthy interactions and prevent negative behaviours. The method is to "Prevent, Teach, Reinforce". This means class material taught through positive interactions, lesson reinforced by referring back to behavioural expectations and evaluating progress.

(*vi*) **Focus on Creative Games** Instead of competitive games and physical activities, the strategy is to develop creative games.

This helps in team building and cooperation and prevents unnecessary competition and boosts the confidence of these children.

(*vii*) **Accomodations and Modification** Since the individual needs of the children with special needs are different, it is essential for the teachers to modify the teaching strategies in order to accommodate the children with disabilities. Therefore constant modification and accommodation is required.

(*viii*) **Professional Courses** Developing more professional courses and teacher certification programs for teaching physical education to children with special needs is essential to popularise the adaptive physical education programme.

Previous Years'

Examination & Other Important Questions

☑ 1 Mark Questions (MCQ)

1. Which of the following organisation not helps the promoting adaptive sports?
(a) Olympics   (b) Deaflympics
(c) Paralympics   (d) b and c only
Ans. *(a)* Olympics

2. The first special Olympic games held in
(a) 1945   (b) 1957
(c) 1968   (d) 1990
Ans. *(c)* 1968

3. Which country has hosted the special Olympics most time
(a) UAE   (b) USA
(c) China   (d) Germany
Ans. *(b)* USA

4. Which of the following games and sports included in special Olympics?
(a) Handball
(b) Judo
(c) Cricket
(d) All of the above
Ans. *(d)* All of the above

5. The first Paralympic games were organised in Rome in
(a) 1945   (b) 1960
(c) 1972   (d) 1998
Ans. *(b)* 1960

6. IPC was formed on 22nd Sepetember, 1989 and its headquarter is located in
(a) Greece   (b) Ireland
(c) Germany   (d) UAE
Ans. *(c)* Germany

7. Logo of Deaflympics is inspired by the sign for
(a) Olympics (b) IPL
(c) IPC   (d) None of these
Ans. *(a)* Olympics

8. Physical activity for children with special needs ....
(a) does not help them to cope with stress, anxiety and depression
(b) helps to change their social behaviour positively
(c) reduces the metabolism of their brain
(d) All of the above
Ans. *(b)* helps to change their social behaviour positively

9. Changing the rules of a game or sport to some extent falls into which one of the following categories of the strategy to make physical activity accessible to children with special needs?
(a) Creation of a specific environment
(b) Adaptive physical education
(c) Assistive technology
(d) Inclusive classroom
Ans. *(b)* Adaptive physical education

☑ 1 Mark Questions (VSA)

1. Why special Olympics are truly inspirational?
Ans. The special Olympics are truly inspirational because they raise awareness of mental and physical disabilities and propagate that everyone can participate in sports.

2. What is the motto of Deaflympics?
Ans. The motto of Deaflympics is 'Per Ludos Aequalitas' meaning 'Equality through sports'.

3. What do you understand by physical activity?
Ans. Physical activity means the movement of the body and use of energy. Walking, running, dancing, swimming, yoga, and gardening are few examples of physical activity.

4. Write any one advantage of physical activity.
Ans. Physical activity enhances the metabolism of brain in the children. It leads to cognitive improvement in children with special needs allowing them to acquire new skills, learn new things and focus on specific goals.

5. Explain the strategy of positive behaviour in brief.
Ans. The strategy of positive behaviour relates to showing a positive attitude and having healthy interactions with the children with special needs.

The teachers should prevent negative behaviours and encourage these children to participate in classroom activities.

6. List down any two strategies to make physical activities accessible for CWSN.

Ans. Strategies to make physical activities accessible for CWSN are
  (*i*) Interest Physical activities must be based on interest, ability and limitation of children with special needs to ensure maximum participation.
  (*ii*) Ability The Physical and mental state of children with special needs shall be considered.

☑ 3 Marks Questions

1. What are the benefits of physical activities for children with special needs? Explain.
  CBSE 2018

Ans. There are a number of benefits of physical activities for children with special needs. *These are as follows*
  (*i*) **Improves Fitness** It strengthens the heart muscles, thereby improving cardiovascular efficiency, lung efficiency and exercise endurance. This helps in controlling repetitive behaviour among disabled children.
  (*ii*) **Develops Social Behaviour** Besides improving fitness, physical activity develops social relationships with other children, teammates and teachers. This brings positive changes in the social behaviour of these children.
  (*iii*) **Makes Improvement in Cognitive Abilities** Physical activity enhances the metabolism of the brain in children. It leads to cognitive improvement in children with special needs allowing them to acquire new skills, learn new things and focus on specific goals.

2. Briefly explain about special Olympic symbol?

Ans. The Special Olympic symbol (logo) is based on the sculpture 'Joy and Happiness to all Children of the World'.

The logo is a symbol of growth, confidence and joy among children and adult with disabilities who are learning coordination, mastery skill, participating in competitions and preparing themselves for richer and more productive lives.

3. What is importance of Paralympics?

Ans. The Paralympic Games are major international multi-sport event involving athletes with various disabilities such as impaired muscle power, impaired passive range of movement, limb deficiency, leg-length difference short stature, hypertonia, ataxia, athetosis, visual and intellectual impairment, blindness, etc.

The Paralympics raise awareness of mental and physical disabilities in the hope of creating a better life for those with disabilities. It therefore serves to change public perception of disabilities in order to provide the Paralympics with better facilities that would drastically improve their quality of life.

4. Explain the strategy of inclusive classrooms. Why is it gaining popularity?

Ans. Inclusive classrooms means including the children with special needs within the normal classrooms where other children study. It requires some changes in existing curriculum so that children with special needs get education along with other children.

This concept is gaining popularity because it helps in changing the outlook of the society. If all the children get education in the same environment then they will understand , interact and cooperate with other. In this way, children with special needs get well accepted in society.

☑ 5 Marks Questions

1. Explain in detail about Paralympic Games.

Ans The Paralympic Games are a major international sports event involving athletes with various disabilities such as mobility disabilities, amputations, blindness and cerebral palsy.

The originator of the Paralympic games is Sir Ludwig Guttmann. He started Paralympic movement that finally developed into Paralympic Games.

The Paralympic Games are governed by the International Paralympic Committee who holds the responsibility of organising the games at an interval of four years. It organises both summer and winter olympics.

The first Paralympic Games were held in Rome in 1960. However, the 'Paralympic' word was officially used in 1988 Summer Olympics, which were held in Seoul. The motto of Paralympic Games is 'Spirit in Motion' which was introduced in 2004 at the Paralympic games Athens.

Its earlier motto was 'Mind, Body and Spirit' which was introduced in 1994. The paralympic games are truly inspirational as the athletes in these games display great determination and courage to overcome mental and physical obstacles.

2. Disuss about 'Deaflympics' in detail.

Ans Deaflympics are the world's second oldest multiple sports after Olympics. The Deaflym pics are an International Olympic Committee sanctioned event at which deaf athletes compete at an international level. The Deaflym pics games are held after every four years.

The first Deaflympics Games were held in Paris in 1924. In that deaflympics, only 148 deaf athletes from nine European countries participated.

From 1924-1965, these games were officially known as the 'International Games for the Deaf'. From 1966-1999, they were called 'World Games for the Deaf'. Since 2001, these games are known as 'Deaflympics'.

In Deaflympics the starter's gun bullhorn commands or refree's whistles are not used, rather flags or any visual signals are used to alert participants.

The motto of Deaflympics is *'Equality through sports'*. The four colours of the logo *i.e.* red, green, yellow and blue, represent the four regional confederations of the International Committee of Sports for the Deaf *viz.* Europe, Asia Pacific, Pan-America and Africa. The circle in the middle represents an eye as deaf people are very visual.

The athletes, to complete in Deaflympics, must have a hearing loss of minimum 55 decible in their better ear.

So, it can be said the Deaflympics provide ample opportunities to persons with hearing disability to participate in elite sports.

3. Explain five strategies to make physical activities accessible for children with special needs.

Ans. *Five strategies to make physical activities accessible for children with special needs are as follows*

(*i*) **Inclusive Classrooms** It means development of education laws in such a way that children with special needs get education within the normal classrooms along with other children so that they are well accepted in society.

(*ii*) **Assistive Technology** It refers to creating devices, tools or equipment that help children with special needs to participate in learning activities. These can be bigger balls, balls with bells, balls attached to strings to bring them back to the students etc.

(*iii*) **Adaptive Physical Education** Depending on the students' disability, a separate, adaptive class or modifications within a game or changing the rules of the game or sport to some extent can help the students in a big way.

(*iv*) **Creating Specific Environment** Students with special needs can be provided with a specific play area with special facilities as needed by them. Loud music or glaring lights often cannot be tolerated by these children; so a lot of natural lighting should be there.

(*v*) **Positive Behaviour** In physical education classes, teachers should show positive behaviour and healthy interactions with such children and avoid negative behaviour. The method is to "Prevent, Teach, Reinforce". This means that material should be taught through positive interactions, the lesson reinforced should be by referring back to behavioural expectations and then only evaluating progress.

CHAPTER 05

Sports and Nutrition

Balanced Diet and Nutrition

A balanced diet is that which contains the proper amount of each nutrient. A balanced diet consists of all essential food constituents i.e. protein, carbohydrates, fats, vitamins and minerals in correct proportion.

Nutrition is the science that deals with food and its uses by the body. Food supplies the energy for every action our body undertakes, from eating bananas to running a race. Food also provides material that our body needs to build and repair its tissues and to regulate the functions of its organs and systems. The chemicals in food which our body needs and are essential for the growth and replacement of tissues are called nutrients.

Macro and Micro Nutrients

Macro Nutrients

The macro nutrients include carbohydrates, proteins and fats.

Carbohydrates

Carbohydrates are the main source of energy in all activities that we do. The elements of carbohydrates are carbon, hydrogen and oxygen. Carbohydrates are organic compounds which are important for our digestive process. They require less water in the diet for being digested. There primary function is to provide energy to the body, especially to the brain and nervous system.

There are two main types of carbohydrates i.e. simple carbohydrates and complex carbohydrates.

Proteins

Proteins are the basic constituents of our cells. They are large molecules, so they cannot get directly into our blood. So, proteins in our food are turned into amino acid by our digestive system. The human body needs 20 different amino acids to maintain good health and normal functioning, out of which 11 are manufactured by the body. So, 9 remaining amino acids sholuld be available from the proteins in our diet. Proteins form tissues, repair the broken tissues, regulate balance of water and oxygen etc. They are body building foods. Foods rich in proteins are eggs, meat, fish and dairy products as well as pulses, nuts and cereals.

Fats

Fats contain hydrogen, carbon and oxygen. These are the most concentrated source of energy in food. Fats have a very high energy content. Foods rich in fats are butter, oil, sausage, cheese, fish, chocolate, olives and nuts. If we do not take enough exercise on a regular basis, we become overweight or even ill. Many fats are unhealthy, such as trans-fats in deep fried foods.

Micro Nutrients

Micro nutrients are vitamins, minerals and secondary plant compounds.

Vitamins

Vitamins are compounds of carbon which are essential for the normal growth and working of the body. They are required in very small quantities. Many of them can be stored in the body for months or even years but others need to be freshly absorbed every day. *There are two groups of vitamins i.e. fat soluble and water soluble :*

(*i*) **Fat Soluble Vitamins** These vitamins are composed of carbon, hydrogen and oxygen and are soluble in fats, such as vitamin A, vitamin D, vitamin E and vitamin K. *The fat soluble vitamins are*

- **Vitamin A** This is essential for normal growth of the body. Deficiency of vitamin A leads to night blindness and also affects the kidneys, nervous system and digestive system.
  Sources are milk, curd, ghee, egg yolk, fish, tomato, papaya, green vegetables, orange, spinach, carrot and pumpkin.

- **Vitamin D** This is essential for the formation of healthy teeth and bones. The presence of this vitamin in the body enables the body to absorb calcium and phosphorus. Its deficiency causes rickets, softness of bones and teeth diseases.
  Sources are egg yolk, fish, sunlight, vegetables, cod liver oil, milk, cream and butter.

- **Vitamin E** This is essential in increasing the fertility among men and women as well as proper functioning of adrenal and sex glands. Its deficiency causes weakness in muscles and heart.
  Sources are green vegetables, sprouts, coconut oil, dry and fresh fruits, milk, meat, butter and maize.

- **Vitamin K** This is helpful in the clotting of blood. Its deficiency causes anaemia and blood does not clot easily.
  Sources are cauliflower, spinach, cabbage, tomato, potato, wheat, egg and meat.

(*ii*) **Water Soluble Vitamins** These vitamins are composed of nitrogen and sulphur and are soluble in water, such as vitamin B complex and vitamin C.

- **Vitamin B Complex** There are 12 vitamins in this group; some of them are B_1, B_2, B_3, B_6 and B_{12}. They are necessary for growth, proper functioning of heart, liver, kidney and maintaining smooth skin. Its deficiency causes Beri-Beri disease, Pellagra and also decreases immunity.
  Sources are wheat, milk, nuts, peas, egg yolk and sprouts.

  - **Vitamin B_1 (Thiamin)** It helps to release energy from foods, promotes normal appetite, and is important in maintaining proper nervous system function.

  - **Vitamin B_2 (Riboflavin)** It helps to release energy from foods, promotes good vision and maintains a healthy skin. It also helps to convert the amino acid tryptophan (which makes up protein) into niacin.

  - **Vitamin B_3 (Niacin)** It works with other B-complex vitamins to metabolise food and provides energy for the body. Vitamin B_3 is involved in energy production, normal enzyme function, digestion, promoting normal appetite, healthy skin and nerves.

  - **Vitamin B_6 (Pyridoxine)** It is a key factor in protein and glucose metabolism as well as in the formation of haemoglobin. Haemoglobin is a component of red blood cells which carries oxygen. Vitamin B_6 is also involved in keeping the lymph nodes and thymus gland healthy.

  - **Vitamin B_{12}** (Cobalamin) It aids in the building of genetic material, production of normal red blood cells, and maintenance of the nervous system.

- **Vitamin C** It is also called Ascorbic acid and is a water-soluble vitamin. It cannot be stored in the body. Most plants and animals can produce their own vitamin C but humans cannot. Vitamin C is needed for proper growth, development, and healing of wounds. It is used to make the collagen tissue for healthy teeth, gums, blood vessels and bones. Deficiency of vitamin C causes scurvy.

Minerals

Minerals contain elements needed by our body in small quantities. But these are essential for proper growth and functioning of the body. A shortage of minerals can have severe effects on health. For instance, a long-term shortage of foods containing iodine in people leads to thyroid gland diseases.

Some of the important minerals are

(*i*) **Iron** It is important for the formation of haemoglobin. Its deficiency leads to anaemia. Its sources are meat, eggs and dry fruits.

(*ii*) **Calcium** It is needed for the formation of strong bones, teeth and also for clotting of blood and muscle contraction. Its deficiency causes rickets and asthma. Its sources are milk, cheese and oranges.

(*iii*) **Phosphorus** It is required for development of strong bones and teeth and also for making energy. Its sources are egg, fish, meat and unpolished rice.

(*iv*) **Potassium** It is important for growth and keeping cells and blood healthy. Its deficiency weakens the muscles of the body. Its sources are carrot, beet root, onion, tomato, orange and mango.

(*v*) **Sodium** It is needed for the proper functioning of the nervous system. Its sources are milk and milk products, meat and eggs.

(*vi*) **Iodine** It is essential for proper thyroid function. Its deficiency causes goitre and sources are seafood and salt.

(*vii*) **Fluorine** It is important to make the enamel (polish) of the teeth hard and prevents dental caries.

(*viii*) **Copper** It is helpful in formation of red blood cells, connective tissue and nerve fibre formation and functioning.

(*ix*) **Zinc** It is required for insulin production and also for functioning of male prostate, digestion and metabolism.

Food components, whether they are nutritive (providing calories) or non-nutritive (not providing calories), are present in a multitude of food and beverages.

Non-nutritive components of food not only provide a flavour to foods but they are also used to preserve foods (in jams or jellies), provide body bulk and texture (in ice-cream and baked goods), enhance other flavours (e.g. salty) and aid in fermentation (in breads and pickles).

The nutritive components of diet are proteins, carbohydrates, fats, vitamins and minerals.

Non-nutritive components do not contribute to the energy, calories or nutrition of the body. Some non-nutritive components are essential for the body while others harm the body. Colour compounds, flavour compounds, food additives, plant compounds, water and roughage or fibre are some non-nutritive components of diet.

Nutritive and Non-Nutritive Components of Diet

Food components, whether they are nutritive (providing calories) or non-nutritive (not providing calories), are present in a multitude of food and beverages. Non-nutritive components of food not only provide a flavour to foods but they are also used to preserve foods (in jams or jellies), provide body bulk and texture (in ice-cream and baked goods), enhance other flavours (e.g. salty) and aid in fermentation (in breads and pickles).

The nutritive components of diet are proteins, carbohydrates, fats, vitamins and minerals.

Non-nutritive components do not contribute to the energy, calories or nutrition of the body. Some non-nutritive components are essential for the body while others harm the body. Colour compounds, flavour compounds, food additives, plant compounds, water and roughage or fibre are some non-nutritive components of diet.

Previous Years'

Examination & Other Important Questions

☑ 1 Mark Questions (MCQ)

1. Scientific name of Vitamin 'C' is
CBSE Term I 2021
(a) Ascorbic acid
(b) Calcium
(c) Retinol
(d) Thiamine
Ans (a) Ascorbic acid

2. The following are macro nutrients, except
CBSE Term I 2021
(a) Carbohydrates   (b) Fat
(c) Vitamins   (d) Proteins
Ans (c) Vitamins

3. The main sources of protein are   **CBSE 2020**
(a) Fish, meat and eggs
(b) Green vegetables
(c) Wheat and rice
(d) Sunlight and water
Ans (a) Fish, meat and eggs

4. Nutrients are the chemicals in food which
....
(a) are needed for replacement of tissues
(b) are essential for growth
(c) our body needs
(d) All of the above
Ans. (d) All of the above

5. Which one of the following is not a macro nutrient?
(a) Fats   (b) Carbohydrates
(c) Roughage   (d) Proteins
Ans. (c) Roughage

6. One function of proteins in our body is to
(a) increase bulk of muscles
(b) improve our endurance
(c) form tissue and repair broken tissues
(d) provide energy for normal activities
Ans. (c) form tissue and repair broken tissues

7. Which of the following is not a form of carbohydrate?
(a) Multiple   (b) Simple
(c) Complex   (d) All of these
Ans. (a) Multiple

8. The mineral .... is required for developing strong bones and teeth.
(a) Potassium
(b) Phosphorous
(c) Sodium
(d) Copper
Ans. (b) Phosphorous

9. Which of the following vitamins is not fat soluble?
(a) B Complex   (b) E
(c) K   (d) A
Ans. (a) B Complex

10. Which of the following vitamins is commonly known as Riboflavin?
(a) B_1 (b) B_2
(c) B_3 (d) B Complex
Ans. (b) B_2

11. Which of the following is a non-nutritive component of diet?
(a) Roughage   (b) Water
(c) Caffeine   (d) All of these
Ans. (d) All of these

12. Assertion (A) Risk of cancer can be reduced by eating more colourful vegetables, fruits and other plant foods that have certain phytochemicals in them.

Reason (R) Non-nutritive components of diet is a part of balanced diet.

In the context of above two statements, which one of the following is correct?

CBSE Term I 2021
Codes
(a) Both A and R are true and R is the correct explanation of A
(b) Both A and R are true, but R is not the correct explanation of A
(c) A is true, but R is false
(d) A is false, but R is true
Ans. (c) A is true, but R is false

☑ 1 Mark Questions (VSA)

1. What are micro nutrients?

All India; Delhi 2016

Ans. Micro nutrients are elements and compounds required in small quantities that control growth and development, cell formation, disease resistance and repair processes of our body.

2. Enlist two sources of calcium and iron separately. **Delhi 2015**

Ans. Calcium—milk, cheese

Iron—meat, eggs

3. Enlist two non-nutritive components of diet. **All India 2015**

Ans. *Non-nutritive components of diet are*

(*i*) Colour compounds (*ii*) Flavour compounds

4. What are vitamins? **All India 2014**

Ans. Vitamins are compounds of carbon which are essential for the normal growth and working of the body. They are required in very small quantities. The important vitamins are A, C, D, E, K and B-complex (B_1, B_2, B_3, B_5, B_6, and B_{12}).

5. What is balanced diet? **Delhi 2014**

or What do you mean by balanced diet?

Ans. A diet that contains sufficient amount of proteins, fats, carbohydrates, minerals, salts, vitamins and water is called balanced diet. A balanced diet is that which contains the proper amount of each nutrient required by our body.

6. What are fats? **CBSE 2013**

Ans. Fats are the energy boosters which provide us with twice as much energy as carbohydrates. We can store extra fat in our body to be used later.

7. What are carbohydrates?

Ans. Carbohydrates are compounds of carbon, hydrogen and oxygen.

Sources of carbohydrates are fruits, milk, vegetables, pulses, bajra, rice, cakes, etc.

8. What do you mean by food and nutrition?

Ans. Food is a mixture of various substances which are essential for life, whereas nutrition is a dynamic process in which the body is made healthy by the consumption of food.

9. What do you mean by components of diet?

Ans. Proteins, fats, carbohydrates, vitamins, minerals and water are called components of diet. These components are composed of various elements such as carbon, hydrogen, oxygen, nitrogen and other macro and micro elements such as calcium, iron, zinc etc.

☑ 3 Marks Questions

1. List down the nutritive component of diet and explain anyone. **CBSE 2020**

Ans. The nutritive components of diet are proteins, carbohydrates, fats, vitamins and minerals. **Carbohydrates** are the main source of energy in all activities that we do. The elements of carbohydrates are carbon, hydrogen and oxygen.

Carbohydrates are organic compounds which are important for our digestive process. They require less water in the diet for being digested.

Their primary function is to provide energy to the body, especially to the brain and nervous system. Their are two main types of carbohydrates *i.e.* simple carbohydrates and complex carbohydrates.

2. What do you understand by non-nutritive component? Elucidate any four non-nutritive component of diet. **CBSE 2020**

Ans. Non-nutritive component of diet do not provide energy or calories. Their main purpose is to make the food smell better, taste better, last longer, and look better.

Some of these component are essential for body while other harms the body. Four non-nutritive components of diet are as follows

(i) **Food Addictives** Certain chemical like benzoic acid, sodium benzoate and other chemicals are used as food preservatives to increase the shelf life of the food.

(ii) **Colour Compounds** Colours are added to the food to make it look attractive and colourful. These are non-nutritive components of diet and excess consumption can be harmful.

(iii) **Plant Compounds** These are derived from plants and mainly used in small amounts. Their excess use may be harmful for body, like caffeine, tea leaves.

(iv) **Water** It is non-nutritive but essential component of diet. It is the main component of blood that carries nutrients to various cells in the body, regulates the body temperature and is significant in the excretion of waste products.

3. What are the nutritive and non-nutritive components of diet? Explain. **Delhi 2017**

Ans. Food components, whether, they are nutritive (providing calories) or non-nutritive (not providing calories), are present in a multiple of food and beverages. Non-nutritive components of food not only provide a flavour to foods, but are also used to preserve foods (in jams or jellies), provide body bulk and texture (in ice-cream and baked goods), enhance other flavours (e.g. salty) and aid in fermentation (in breads and pickles).

The nutritive components of diet are proteins, carbohydrates, fats, vitamins and minerals.

Non-nutritive components do not contribute to the energy, calories or nutrition of the body. Some non-nutritive components are essential for the body while others harm the body. Colour compounds, flavour compounds, food additives, plant compounds, water and roughage or fibre are some non-nutritive components of diet.

4. Write briefly about proteins as an essential component of diet. **Delhi 2016**

or What are proteins? Discuss.

Ans. Proteins are the basic structure of all living cells. These are complex organic compounds. Protein is a chain of amino acids that contain carbon, oxygen, hydrogen and nitrogen.

There are two types of proteins
(*i*) Vegetable proteins (*ii*) Animal proteins

Sources All meat and other animal products are sources of proteins. The best sources are eggs, milk, meat, poultry, milk products, beans, etc.

5. Briefly explain the functions and resources of fat soluble vitamins. **Delhi 2015**

Ans. The vitamins that are soluble in fats are called fat soluble vitamins. They are vitamin A, D, E and K.

Functions

- **Vitamin A** This is essential for normal growth of the body. Deficiency of vitamin A leads to night blindness and also affects the kidneys, nervous system and digestive system.
  Sources are milk, curd, ghee, egg yolk, fish, tomato, papaya, green vegetables, orange, spinach, carrot and pumpkin.
- **Vitamin D** This is essential for the formation of healthy teeth and bones. The presence of this vitamin in the body enables it to absorb calcium and phosphorus. Its deficiency causes rickets, softness of bones, teeth diseases.
  Sources are egg yolk, fish, sunlight, vegetables, cod liver oil, milk, cream, butter.
- **Vitamin E** This is essential in increasing the fertility among men and women as well as proper functioning of adrenal and sex glands. Its deficiency causes weakness in muscles and heart.
  Sources are green vegetables, sprouts, coconut oil, dry and fresh fruits, milk, meat, butter, maize.
  Vitamin K This is helpful in the clotting of blood. Its deficiency causes anaemia and blood do not clot easily.
  Sources are cauliflower, spinach, cabbage, tomato, potato, wheat, egg and meat.

6. What are vitamins? Name the types of vitamins.

or Vitamins are very essential for working of the body and are divided into two groups. Explain about them. **All India 2015**

Ans. Vitamins are compounds of carbon. These protect us from various diseases and are essential for general growth and development of our body.

Types of Vitamins There are various vitamins such as A, C, D, E, K and B-complex ($B_1, B_2, B_3,$ B_5, B_6, B_7, B_9 and B_{12}). *There are two groups of vitamins*

Fat Soluble Vitamins Fat soluble vitamins are those vitamins which are soluble in fat. *These vitamins are A, D, E and K which are given below*

- Vitamin A is essential for normal growth, proper functioning of nervous system and digestive system.
- Vitamin D is essential for healthy bones and teeth.
- Vitamin E increases fertility and ensures proper functioning of the glands.
- Vitamin K helps in clotting of blood.

Water Soluble Vitamins These vitamins are soluble in water. These contain the elements nitrogen and sulphur.

These vitamins are B complex and C.

- Vitamin B complex consists of various groups of vitamins namely $B_1, B_2, B_3, B_6,$ and B_{12}. They are necessary for proper growth and functioning of various organs of the body.
- Vitamin C is essential for maintenance of ligaments, tissues, tendons and strong blood vessels.

7. What are fats? Write a detailed note on its types. Also mention its importance in the proper functioning of the body. **CBSE 2012**

Ans. Fats contain carbon, hydrogen and oxygen. These are the most concentrated source of energy in food.

Sources of Fats Animal products such as meat, poultry and dairy products such as milk, cream, cheese, butter and ice-cream, peanuts, olive oil, etc.

Types Fats can be classified according to their structures. Different types of fats have different characteristics and these react in different ways inside the body. There are three different groups of fats in the diet, which are saturated, poly-unsaturated and mono-unsaturated fats. The intake of saturated fats increases the chances of heart diseases due to the increase of cholesterol in the blood.

Importance

- Fats keep us warm and give protection to organs.
- Fats also help in production of hormones.
- Fatty acids provide the raw materials which help in control of blood pressure, blood clotting and other body functions.
- Fats help in transportation of fat soluble vitamins such as A, D, E and K.
- Fats maintain skin and hair.

8. Discuss the functions and sources of fats.

Ans. Fats are an essential ingredient of food. All fats are compounds of carbon, hydrogen and oxygen.

Functions of Fats

- They provide heat and energy to the body.
- They also help in regulation of body temperature.
- They are considered better than carbohydrates as sources of energy.
- Fats give protection to organs.

Sources of Fats

- **Animal Sources** We get various products from animals such as ghee, butter, curd, fish oil, milk, meat and eggs.
- **Vegetable Sources** We also get fats from various vegetables such as dry fruits, coconut, soybean, foodgrains, mustard oil and cotton seeds.

9. Mention the uses of any two minerals in our diet.

Ans. (*i*) **Iodine** It is essential for proper thyroid gland function. Its deficiency causes goitre. Its sources are seafood and common table salt.

(*ii*) **Calcium** It is helpful in the formation of teeth and bones. It helps in clotting of blood. Its deficiency causes rickets and asthma. Milk, cheese, oranges and green vegetables have a rich amount of calcium.

10. What is balanced diet? Elaborate the important nutrients/elements of balanced diet.

Ans. **Balanced Diet** A balanced diet is that which contains the proper amounts of each nutrient. A balanced diet consists of all essential food constituents i.e. protein, carbohydrates, fats, vitamins and minerals in correct proportion.

Elements

(*i*) **Carbohydrates** These are our main sources of energy.

(*ii*) **Proteins** These provide essential growth as well as repairing muscles and other body tissues.

(*iii*) **Fats** These are the sources of energy.

(*iv*) **Vitamins** These play an important role in many chemical processes in the body.

(*v*) **Minerals** These are essential for proper growth and functioning of our body.

(*vi*) **Water** It is essential for normal body functions. It serves as a vehicle for carrying other nutrients.

☐ 5 Marks Questions

1. Explain macro-nutrients and their role in our diet. **CBSE 2019**

Ans. The macro-nutrients in the diet consist of carbohydrates, proteins and fats. Each of these macro-nutrients plays an important role in the diet, *as given below*

(*i*) **Carbohydrates** They are needed to provide energy for all activities. They are stored mostly in the muscles and the liver. Complex carbohydrates are found in foods such as pasta, bagels, whole grain breads and rice. These foods also provide energy, fibre, vitamins and minerals.

(*ii*) **Proteins** They are important for muscle growth and repair of body tissues. Proteins are found in meat, eggs, fish, soya bean, lentils and many other food items. Athletes as well as body builders need only a little bit of extra protein to support muscle growth. Athletes can meet this increased requirement by eating more total calories (i.e. by eating more food).

(*iii*) **Fats** They provide the highest concentration of energy of all the nutrients. Saturated fats are found primarily in animal sources such as meat, egg yolks, yogurt, cheese, butter and milk. Unsaturated fats include monounsaturated and polyunsaturated fats, which are typically found in plant food sources.

2. Explain any five essential elements of diet. **Delhi 2014**

Ans. There are many nutrients in the food. These are known as elements. *Essential elements of our diet are*

(*i*) **Carbohydrates** These are the compounds of carbon, hydrogen and oxygen.

Sources Fruits, milk, vegetables, pulses, bajra, rice, cakes, etc.

Functions The main function of carbohydrates is to provide energy to the body, brain and nervous system.

(*ii*) **Proteins** Proteins are a chain of amino acids that contain carbon, oxygen, hydrogen and nitrogen.

Sources Eggs, milk, meat, beans, animal products, etc.

Functions Proteins are the main components of muscles, organs and glands. The cells of muscles and ligaments are maintained with protein and proteins are used for the growth and development of children.

(*iii*) **Fats** Fats contain carbon, hydrogen and oxygen.

Sources Animal products, milk, cream, cheese, butter, olive oil, etc.

Functions Fats are a source of energy. They are important for the proper functioning of the body. Fatty acids provide the raw materials which help in control of blood pressure.

(*iv*) **Vitamins** Vitamins are compounds of carbon. The important vitamins are A, C, D E, K and B- complex (B_1, B_2, B_3, B_5, B_6, B_7, B_9 and B_{12}).

Sources Milk, butter, eggs, green vegetables, exposure to sunlight, oil, nuts, seeds, fish, amla, etc.

Functions Vitamins play an important role in many chemical processes in the body. Vitamins are essential for metabolism of fat and carbohydrate and are needed for healthy skin. They are helpful in red blood cell production.

(*v*) **Minerals** Minerals are iron, calcium, phosphorus, sodium, iodine, copper, chloride, etc.

Sources Eggs, milk, meat, green vegetables, pulses, fish, salts, tea and coffee, etc.

Functions Minerals are essential for proper growth of the body. Calcium is needed for strong teeth and bones. It is also essential for proper thyroid function.

(*vi*) **Water** Water is an important element of balanced diet.

Source Nature.

Functions Water helps in the digestive system. It regulates the body temperature and carries nutrients to cells.

3. "Vitamins are essential for our metabolic process". What happens if we devoid our diet of vitamins? **CBSE 2012**

Ans. Vitamins are required by the body for proper growth and development. *The following may happen if we remove vitamins from our diet*

- In the absence of vitamin A, there may be night-blindness.
- Deficiency of vitamin B causes Beri-Beri disease.
- Deficiency of vitamin C causes Scurvy.
- Deficiency of vitamin E causes weakness in heart and muscles.
- Deficiency of vitamin K causes Anaemia.
- In addition, deficiency of vitamins in the body affects the working of the organs, nervous system and digestive system adversely.
- Their presence is necessary for maintaining healthy teeth and bones as well as overall health.

CHAPTER 06

Test and Measurement in Sports

In physical education, there is a need to **test** content knowledge, fitness levels, motor skills as well as attitudes and feelings related to physical activity. Many types of tests may be effectively utilised in physical education; for example a shuttle run can measure agility, a 40 yard sprint test running speed, a 12 minute run is commonly used to test cardiovascular endurance and so on. Before conducting a test, the **measurements** for the test are fixed. These measurements are quantitative in nature and can be related to size, height, weight, vital capacity, achievements etc. Measurement is a specific score given by an expert every time on applying a test. Each score tells about the use of a test once. Every time a test is used, it will have a score called measurement.

Fitness Test - SAI Khelo India Fitness Test in School

Fitness defines the ability to perform physical activity and encompasses a wide range of abilities. Each activity and sports requires a specific set of skills, and so being fit for an activity or a sport does not necessarily make a person fit for another. Fitness is generally divided into specific fitness categories or components, and each can be tested and trained individually.

Age Group 5-8 Years/ Class 1 To 3

At Primary class 1-3, children should acquire Fundamental Movement Skills (FMS) leaving the learning of specific physical activities to later stages. FMS provide the building blocks for many physical activities, such as playing games, dance, and sport.

Following are the abilities of children in class 1-3 which need to be measured and tracked and are important for controlling the body in various situations:

- Body Composition (BMI)
- Balance (Flamingo Balance)
- Coordination (Plate Tapping)

Body Composition (BMI)

Body Composition refers primarily to the distribution of muscle and fat in the body. Body size such as height, lengths and girths are also grouped under this component. The test performed is Body Mass Index (BMI), which is calculated from body Weight (W) and Height (H) such as

$$BMI = W/(H \times H)$$

Where: W = body weight in kilograms and

H = height in meters.

The higher the score usually indicating higher levels of body fat.

Equipments Required

- Flat, Clean surface, Weighing
- Machine, Stadiometer/Measuring Tape pasted on a wall

Procedure

Measuring Height Accurately

- Remove the participant's shoes, bulky clothing, and hair ornaments, and unbraid hair that interferes with the measurement.
- Take the height measurement on flooring that is not carpeted and against a flat surface such as a wall with no molding.
- Have the participant stand with feet flat, together, and back against the wall. Make sure legs are straight, arms are at sides, and shoulders are level.
- Make sure the participant is looking straight ahead and that the line of sight is parallel with the floor.
- Use a flat headpiece to form a right angle with the wall and lower the headpiece until it firmly touches the crown of the head.
- Then, use a metal tape to measure from the base on the floor to the marked measurement on the wall to get the height measurement.

Measuring Weight Accurately

- Use a digital scale. Avoid using bathroom scales that are spring loaded. Place the scale on firm flooring such as tile or wood rather than carpet.
- Have the participant remove shoes and heavy clothing, such as sweaters.
- Have the participant stand with both feet in the center of the scale.
- Record the weight to the nearest decimal fraction e.g. 30.6 kilograms.

Flamingo Balance Test

Purpose It measures ability to balance successfully on a single leg. This single leg balance test assesses the strength of the leg, pelvic, and trunk muscle as well as static balance.

Flamingo

Equipments Required

- Non- Slippery even surface
- Stopwatch
- Can be done on just standing on beam

Procedure

- Stand on the beam. Keep balance by holding the instructor's hand (if required to start).
- While balancing on the preferred leg, the free leg is flexed at the knee and the foot of this leg held close to the buttocks.
- Start the watch as the instructor lets go of the participant/subject.
- Pause the stopwatch each time the subject loses balance (either by falling off the beam or letting goes of the foot being held).
- Resume over, again timing until they lose balance. Count the number of falls in 60 seconds of balancing.
- If there are more than 15 falls in the first 30 seconds, the test is terminated.

Plate Tapping Test

Purpose- It measures speed and coordination of limb movement of children.

Equipments Required

- Table (adjustable height)
- 2 yellow discs (20cm diameter)
- Rectangle (30 x 20 cm)
- Stopwatch

Procedure

- If possible, the table height should be adjusted so that the subject is standing comfortably in front of the discs. The two yellow discs are placed with their centers 60 cm apart on the table. The rectangle is placed equidistant between both discs.
- The non-preferred hand is placed on the rectangle. The subject moves the preferred hand back and forth between the discs over the hand in the middle as quickly as possible.
- This action is repeated for 25 full cycles (50 taps).

Age Group 9-18+ Years/ Class 4 To 12

For Class 4 to 12, it is important for students to have an overall physical fitness. The following components are to be considered in Physical Health and Fitness Profile

- Body Composition (BMI)
- Speed (50 mt speed test)
- Cardiovascular Endurance (600 mt Run/Walk)
- Flexibility (Sit and Reach Test)
- Strength (Abdominal Partial Curl-up, Push Ups for Boys, Modified Push Ups for Girls)

Note The procedure of Body Composition (BMI) for age group 9-18 + years is same as age group 3-4 years.

50 M Speed Test

- **Purpose** To measure speed.
- **Procedure** The youth is asked to run 50 metres from a standing start and the time is recorded nearest to one-tenths of a second.

600 M Run/Walk

- **Purpose** To measure endurance.
- **Procedure** The youth is asked to run and/or walk for 600 metres and the time is recorded in minutes and seconds. This can be run in an open field or the inside track of an athletic field, by marking the distances appropriately.

Sit and Reach

- **Purpose** This test is a common measure of flexibility and specifically measures the flexibility of the lower back and hamstring muscles.

Strength Test

1. Abdominal Partial Curl

- **Purpose** This test measures abdominal strength and endurance, which is important in back support and core stability.
- **Procedure** The starting position is lying on the back with the knees flexed and feet 25 cm from the buttocks. The feet are not to be held or rest against an object. The arms are extended and are rested on the thighs. The head is in a neutral position. The subject curls up with a slow controlled movement, until the subject's shoulders come off the mat two inches, then back down again. One complete curl-up is completed every three seconds (1.5 seconds up and 1.5 seconds down, with no hesitation), and are continued until exhaustion, meaning that till the subject cannot maintain the rhythm. There is no pause in the up or down position; the curl-ups should be continuous with the abdominal muscles engaged throughout. Record the total number of curl ups completed. Only correctly performed curl ups should be counted.

2. Push Ups (Boys)

- **Purpose** This test measures upper body strength and endurance.
- **Procedure** A standard push-up begins with the hands and toes touching the floor, the body and legs in a straight line, feet slightly apart, the arms at shoulder width apart, extended and at a right angle to the body. Keeping the back and knees straight, the subject lowers the body to a predetermined point, to touch some other object, or until there is a 90-degree angle at the elbows, then returns back to the starting position with the arms extended. This action is repeated, and the test continues until exhaustion, or until the subject can do no more in rhythm or has reached the targeted number of push-ups. Record the number of correctly completed push-ups.

3. Modified Push Ups (Girls)

* **Purpose** This test is used to measure upper body strength, endurance and trunk stability.
* **Procedure** The subject lies face down on the mat. The test begins by clapping the hands together behind the back once, then the hands are brought back next to the shoulders and a normal straight-leg push-up is completed with elbows completely straight in the up position. One hand is then used to touch the back of the other hand before lowering the body again. The subject ends the cycle back in the face-down position on the mat. The timing starts when the subject first claps the hands behind the back, then continues for 40 seconds.

  Record the total number of correctly completed push-ups that were performed in 40 seconds.

Basal Metabolic Rate (BMR)

Basal Metabolic Rate (BMR) is the number of calories our body needs to accomplish its most basic (basal) life-sustaining functions such as breathing, circulation, nutrient processing and cell production. Around 60-75% of our daily calories are burned during these processes. It is the rate of one's metabolism when waking up in the morning after fasting during sleep.

The BMR is enough energy for the brain and central nervous system, heart, kidneys, liver, lungs, muscles, sex organs, and skin to function properly.

People who are overweight or obese do not necessarily have a slow BMR. In fact, their BMR is usually faster to accommodate for extra fat and for their body to work harder to perform normal body functions.

Building lean muscle mass can increase BMR, but there is a limit for both men and women as to how much lean muscle mass can be built. Some supplements may increase BMR, but also only to a limit, and they may have serious side effects.

Computing Basal Metabolic Rate (BMR)

One popular way to estimate BMR is through the Harris-Benedict formula, which takes into account weight, height, age and gender such as

For Women

BMR = 65 + (9.6 × weight in kg) + (1.8 × height in cm) − (4.7 × age in years)

For Men

BMR = 66 + (13.7 × weight in kg) + (5 × height in cm) − (6.8 × age in years)

Rikli and Jones— Senior Citizen Fitness Test

Rikli and Jones prepared various physical fitness tests for senior citizens in 2001. Senior citizens can't do exhaustive workouts however fitness is very important even in old age. These tests are designed to access the functional fitness of older adults with the help of simple activities like getting up from a chair, walking, bending and stretching. These tests are safe, enjoyable and meet scientific standards of reliability and validity. That is why easy tests prepared for different body parts are given. *These are*

1. Chair Stand Test for Lower Body Strength

The Chair Stand Test is similar to a squat test to measure leg strength. This test is part of the senior fitness test protocol and is designed to test the functional fitness of seniors.

* **Purpose** This test assesses leg strength and endurance of senior citizens.
* **Equipment Required** A straight or folding chair without arm rests (seat 17 inches/ 44 cm high) and stopwatch.

2. Arm Curl Test for Upper Body Strength

The Arm Curl Test is a test to measure the upper body strength of senior citizens or old people.

- **Purpose** This test measures upper body strength and endurance.
- **Equipment Required** 5 pound weight for women, 8 pound weight for men, a chair without arm rests, stopwatch.

3. Chair Sit and Reach Test for Lower Body Flexibility

The Chair Sit and Reach Test is part of the senior fitness test protocol, and is designed to test the functional fitness of seniors. It is a variation of the traditional sit and reach flexibility test.

- **Purpose** This test measures lower body flexibility.
- **Equipment Required** Ruler, a chair with straight back or folding chair (17 inch/ 44 cm high).

4. Back Scratch Test for Upper Body Flexibility

The shoulder stretch is a simple flexibility test to determine if the hands can be brought together behind the back particularly the shoulders.

This test is part of the fitness programme as an alternative to the back saver sit and reach test.

- **Purpose** This test measures upper arm and shoulder girdle flexibility.
- **Equipment Required** None

5. Eight Foot Up and Go Test for Agility

The Eight Foot Up and Go Test is a coordination and agility test for the elderly which is part of the senior fitness test protocol.

- **Purpose** This test measures speed, agility and balance while moving.
- **Equipment Required** Stopwatch, straight back or folding chair (seat 17 inches/44 cm high) cone marker, measuring tape, area clear of obstacles.

6. Six Minute Walk Test for Aerobic Endurance

The Six Minute Walk Test is a part of the senior fitness test protocol and is designed to test the functional fitness of seniors.

It is an adaptation of the Cooper 12- minutes run for people who use orthopaedic devices when walking as well as people who have difficulty in balancing.

- **Purpose** This test measures aerobic fitness or aerobic endurance.
- **Equipment Required** Measuring tape to mark out the track distances, stopwatch and chairs positioned for testing.

Previous Years'

Examination & Other Important Questions

📑 1 Mark Questions (MCQ)

1. The age group of children and youth is
CBSE Term I 2021
(a) 5-25 yrs   (b) 5-17 yrs
(c) 5-21 yrs   (d) 5-15 yrs
Ans. (a) 5-25 yrs

2. Ankit lives with his grandfather who is 65 years old and leads a sedentary lifestyle. Ankit is worried about his health. He would like to test his grandfather's functional fitness. Which test should Ankit administrate to check his grandfather's lower body flexibility?
CBSE Term I 2021
(a) Chair stand test
(b) Arm curl test
(c) Back scratch test
(d) Chair sit and reach test
Ans (d) Chair sit and reach test

3. Sit and Reach Test is conducted to measure **CBSE 2020**
(a) Flexibility   (b) Motor Fitness
(c) Endurance   (d) Speed
Ans (a) Flexibility

4. FMS provides the building blocks. For many physical activites such as
(a) playing games   (b) Dance
(c) sports   (d) All of these
Ans. (d) All of these

5. Purpose of plate tapping test is
(a) Measures speed   (b) Coordination of limb
(c) both (a) and (b)   (d) None of these
Ans. (c) both (a) and (b)

6. What is equipments required for Flaming Balance test?
(a) Stopwatch   (b) Table
(c) Disc   (d) Measuring Tape
Ans. (a) Stopwatch

7. Which of following test is the strength test?
(a) Partial Curl up
(b) Push ups for boys
(c) Modified push ups for girl
(d) All of the above
Ans. (d) All of the above

8. In the motor fitness test, the 600 metres run/ walk measures ....
(a) speed and agility   (b) power
(c) endurance   (d) All of these
Ans. (c) endurance

9. People who are overweight or obese do not necessarity have a slow.
(a) FCI   (b) BMR
(c) FMS   (d) None of these
Ans. (b) BMR

10. What is the height of the chair's seat above the ground in the Senior Citizen Chair Stand test?
(a) 17 cm   (b) 44 cm
(c) Not specified   (d) None of these
Ans. (b) 44 cm

11. In the Arm Curl Test for upper body strength, if a woman of 68 years is able to complete 19 curl ups in 30 seconds, her fitness level will be classified as ....
(a) below average   (b) average
(c) above average   (d) phenomenal
Ans. (c) above average

12. In the Chair Sit and Reach Test for Senior Citizens, the distance measured is between the .... and the ....
(a) wrist, toes
(b) fingers, heels
(c) tip of the finger tips, toes
(d) None of the above
Ans. (c) tip of the finger tips, toes

13. The Back Stretch Test for upper body flexibility is done in a .... position.
(a) standing
(b) sitting on the floor
(c) sitting in a chair
(d) Either (b) or (c)
Ans. (a) standing

14. If a male Senior Citizen of 65 years completes two trials in the Eight Foot Up and Go Test in 5.3 and 4.2 seconds respectively, his agility will be classified as ....

(a) below average   (b) average
(c) above average   (d) extremely poor

Ans. *(c)* above average

15. The Six Minute Walk Test for Senior Citizens measures ....

(a) overall physical fitness (b) walking fitness
(c) lower body fitness   (d) None of these

Ans. *(d)* None of the above

☑ 1 Mark Questions (VSA)

1. Your grandmother feels she has reduced her upper body flexibility and therefore she wants to test herself. Which test would you suggest her? **All India 2017; Delhi 2015**

Ans. I would suggest to my grandmother to take the Back stretch Test for upper body flexibility under the Rikli and Jones Senior Citizen Fitness Tests.

2. Which test would you suggest for your grandmother to test lower body flexibility?
All India 2015

Ans. I would suggest Chair Sit and Reach Test for my grandmother to test lower body flexibility.

3. Which motor quality does a senior citizen lack who finds difficulty in tying the shoe laces while sitting on a chair?

Ans. The senior citizen lacks lower body flexibility.

4. What is the purpose of the Partial Curl Up Test?

Ans. The purpose of the Partial Curl Up Test is to measure abdominal strength and endurance, which is important in back support and core stability.

5. How is the scoring done for the Sit and Reach Test?

Ans. In the Sit and Reach Test, each subject is given three trials. The highest score nearest to a cm is recorded and 25 cm are subtracted from the recorded reading to obtain the flexibility score, which is compared with the standards to decide the flexibility.

6. What is a test in sports?

Ans. Test in sports means content knowledge, fitness levels, motor skills as well as attitudes and feelings required for the particular sport.

☑ 3 Marks Questions

1. Describe in detail 'Eight Foot Up and Go Test' for agility. **All India 2016**

or Explain the procedure for Eight Foot Up and Go Test.

Ans. The Eight Foot Up and Go Test is a coordination and agility test for the elderly. The purpose of this test is to measure speed, agility and balance while moving. *The procedure is*

(i) Place the chair next to a wall for safety and the marker 8 feet in front of the chair. Clear the path between the chair and the marker.

(ii) The subject should start fully seated, hands resting on the knees and feet flat on the ground.

(iii) On the command 'go', the stopwatch is started and the subject stands and walks (no running is allowed) as quickly as possible as to and around the cone, returning to the chair to sit down.

(iv) The score is the better time of two trials to the nearest 1/10th sec.

2. What is the purpose of the Sit and Reach Test? Describe the procedure for carrying out this test in point form.

Ans. The purpose of the Sit and Reach Test is to measure flexibility, and specifically measure the flexibility of the lower back and hamstring muscles.

The procedure for carrying out this test is as follows

(i) The subject is asked to removes shoes and place the feet against the testing box while sitting on the floor with straight knees.

(ii) Now the subject is asked to place one hand on top of the other so that the middle fingers of both hands are together at the same length. The tester's hand is kept on the knees of the subject to not allow any bending of the knees.

(iii) The subject is instructed to lean forwards and place the hands over the measuring scale lying on the top of the box with its 25 cm mark coinciding with the front edge of the testing box.

(*iv*) Then the subject is asked to slide the hands along the measuring scale as far as possible without bouncing and to hold the farthest position for at least one second. This procedure is carried out three times and the best result of the three is taken as the score.

3. Explain the procedure for carrying out the Partial Curl Up Test in point form.

Ans. *The procedure for carrying out the Partial Curl Up Test is as follows*

(*i*) The starting position is lying on the back with the knees flexed and feet 25 cm from the buttocks. The feet are not to be held or rest against an object. The arms are extended and are rested on the thighs. The head is in a neutral position.

(*ii*) The subject curls up with a slow controlled movement, until the subject's shoulders come off the mat two inches, then back down again.

(*iii*) One complete curl-up is completed every three seconds (1.5 seconds up and 1.5 seconds down, with no hesitation), and are continued until exhaustion, meaning that till the subject cannot maintain the rhythm.

(*iv*) There is no pause in the up or down position; the curl-ups should be continuous with the abdominal muscles engaged throughout. The total number of curl ups completed till exhaustion is the score of the subject.

4. Give the names of the tests designed by Rikli and Jones for senior citizen fitness and state what each test is used to test.

Ans. *The tests designed by Rikli and Jones for senior citizen fitness are*

(*i*) Chair Stand Test for lower body strength.

(*ii*) Arm Curl Test for upper body strength and endurance.

(*iii*) Chair Sit and Reach Test for lower body flexibility.

(*iv*) Back Stretch Test for upper body flexibility.

(*v*) Eight Foot Up and Go Test for coordination and agility.

(*vi*) Six Minute Walk Test for aerobic fitness and endurance.

5. What is the usefulness of Back Scratch Test for senior citizens?

Ans. The usefulness of the Back Scratch Test for senior citizens is to assess the upper body flexibility, particularly the shoulders.

The shoulder stretch is a simple flexibility test to determine if the hands can be brought together behind the back particularly the shoulders. This test is part of the fitness programme as an alternative to the back saver sit and reach test.

6. Describe the purpose and procedure of Six Minute Walk Test for aerobic endurance.

Ans. **Purpose** This test measures aerobic fitness and endurance of senior citizens.

Procedure The walking course is laid out in a 50 yard (45.72 m) rectangular area (dimension 45×5 *yards)* with cones placed at regular intervals to indicate distance walked.

The aim of this test is to walk as quickly as possible for six minutes to cover as much ground as possible. Subjects are to set their own pace (a preliminary trial is useful to practise pacing) and are allowed to stop for a rest if they desire.

7. Below given is the BMI data of a school's health check

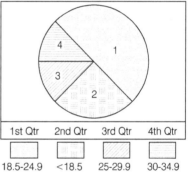

On the basis of the above data answer the following questions : **CBSE QB 2021**

(i) In which category does the major student population falls into?

   (a) Obese   (b) Normal weight

   (c) Under weight   (d) Over weight

(ii) The school has to develop an activity based program to decrease the number of:

   (a) ☐   (b) ☐

   (c) ☐   (d) ☐

(iii) Which category is related to underweight?

   (a) ☐   (b) ☐

   (c) ☐   (d) ☐

Ans. (i) - (a),   (ii) - (d),   (iii) - (b)

8. Rajesh went to an old age home on the occasion of his birthday. At that time all the inmates in the home were assembled in one place. When he enquired, they replied that they have a physical fitness test.

(i) Give any one standard physical fitness test for senior citizen
   (a) Push ups
   (b) Standing Broad jump
   (c) Zig zag run
   (d) Eight foot up and go test

(ii) Chair stand test is used for measuring the
   (a) Lower body strength   (b) Upper body test
   (c) Aerobic fitness   (d) Anaerobic fitness

(iii) The weight of dumbbells in Arm Curl test for men is
   (a) 5 pounds   (b) 4 pounds
   (c) 8 pounds   (d) 10 pounds

Ans. (i) - (d),   (ii) - (a),   (iii) - (c)

9. Sports Minister, Mr. Kiren Rijuju has launched many sports schemes in India. Among these, one of the best schemes is Khelo India. Mr. Kannan, father of Kartik approached the PE teacher and enquired about the fitness levels of the students.

PE teacher replied that Khelo India consisted of physical fitness tests for school children and they were analysing students fitness through these tests.

(i) To measure Lower body flexibility fitness, which one of the following is best?
   (a) Harvard Step Test
   (b) Sit and reach test
   (c) Barrow fitness test
   (d) General fitness test

(ii) Rikli Jones test is conducted on
   (a) Children   (b) Adults
   (c) Adolescent   (d) Senior Citizens

(iii) Which method should he follow to improve the jump?
   (a) Flexibility   (b) Explosive power
   (c) Push-ups   (d) Shuttle run

Ans. (i) - (b),   (ii) - (d),   (iii) - (b)

🗹 5 Marks Questions

1. Describe the procedure for administering the Rikli and Jones Senior Citizen Fitness Test. **CBSE 2014**

Ans. The Rikli and Jones Senior Citizen Fitness Test for assessing the functional fitness of older adults describes easy to understand and effective tests to measure aerobic fitness, strength and flexibility using minimal and inexpensive equipment.

These test items involve common activities such as getting up from a chair, walking, lifting, bending and stretching.

The tests were developed to be safe and enjoyable for older adults while still meeting scientific standards for reliability and validity.

The tests are
(*i*) Chair Stand Test – testing lower body strength
(*ii*) Arm Curl Test – testing upper body strength
(*iii*) Chair Sit and Reach Test – testing lower body flexibility test
(*iv*) Back Stretch Test – testing upper body flexibility test
(*v*) Eight Foot Up and Go Test – testing agility test
(*vi*) Six minute Walk Test – aerobic fitness and endurance

2. In the Fitness Test, what do the Push Up Tests measure? Describe the procedure for carrying out this test for girls in point form.

Ans. In the Motor Fitness Test, the Push Up Tests measure upper body strength, endurance and trunk stability.

The procedure for carrying out this test for girls are follows
(*i*) The subject lies face down on the mat.
(*ii*) The test begins by clapping the hands together behind the back once.
(*iii*) Now the hands are brought back next to the shoulders and a normal straight-leg push-up is completed with elbows completely straight in the up position.
(*iv*) Now one hand is used to touch the back of the other hand before lowering the body again.
(*v*) The subject ends the cycle back in the face-down position on the mat.
(*vi*) The timing starts when the subject first claps the hands behind the back and continues for 40 seconds. The total number of completed push-ups that were performed in 40 seconds is counted as the score.

3. Explain the Arm Curl Test for upper body strength for senior citizens.

Ans. The Arm Curl Test is a test of upper body strength. The purpose of this test is to measure upper body strength and endurance. The subject has to do as many arm curls as possible in 30 sec. This test is conducted on the dominant arm side (or stronger side).

Its procedure is

(*i*) The subject sits on the chair holding the weight (8 pounds for men / 5 pounds for women) in the hand using a suitcase grip (palm facing towards the body) with the arm in a vertically down position beside the chair.

(*ii*) The upper arm is held close to the body so that only the lower arm is moving.

(*iii*) The subject curls the arm up through a full range of motion, gradually turning the palm up (flexion with supination).

(*iv*) Then the arm is lowered through the full range of motion, gradually return to the starting position. The arm must be fully bent and then fully straightened at the elbow.

(*v*) Repeat this action as many times as possible within 30 sec.

(*vi*) The score is the total number of controlled arm curls performed in 30 sec.

4. What is the procedure of measuring height in Body Mass Index?

Ans. The procedure of measuring height accurately in BMI is given below

- Remove the participant's shoes, bulky clothing, and hair ornaments, and unbraid hair that interferes with the measurement.
- Take the height measurement on flooring that is not carpeted and against a flat surface such as a wall with no molding.
- Have the participant stand with feet flat, together, and back against the wall. Make sure legs are straight, arms are at sides, and shoulders are level.
- Make sure the participant is looking straight ahead and that the line of sight is parallel with the floor.
- Take the measurement while the participant stands with head, shoulders, buttocks, and heels touching the flat surface (wall). Depending on the overall body shape of the participant, all points may not touch the wall.
- Use a flat headpiece to form a right angle with the wall and lower the headpiece until it firmly touches the crown of the head.
- Make sure the measurer's eyes are at the same level as the headpiece.
- Lightly mark where the bottom of the headpiece meets the wall.
- Then, use a metal tape to measure from the base on the floor to the marked measurement on the wall to get the height measurement.
- Accurately record the height to the nearest 0.1 centimeter.

CHAPTER 07

Physiology and Injuries in Sports

Physiological Factors Determining Components of Physical Fitness

In physiology, we study how our organs, systems, tissues, cells and molecules within cells work and how their functions are put together to maintain our internal environment. "Physiology is the study of how the human body functions." Physiology is very essential to understand how to attain physical fitness in order to enhance the performance in sports.

To understand the physiological factors, the components of physical fitness have to be understood.

The components of physical fitness are as follows

(*i*) **Muscular Strength** One of the basic requirements for success in all movements is muscular strength. It may be defined as the maximum force or tension a muscle or a muscle group can exert against a resistance. The development of strength is specific to the muscle or muscles involved in a particular activity.

(*ii*) **Power** Power is the ability of the body to release maximum muscle contraction in the shortest possible time.

(*iii*) **Speed** It is the rapidity with which one repeats successive movements of the same pattern. It may also be defined as the ability of a person to move quickly through a short distance.

(*iv*) **Muscular Endurance** It may be defined as the ability of a muscle or muscle group to perform repeated contractions against a resistance / load or to sustain contraction for an extended period of time with less discomfort and more rapid recovery.

(*v*) **Agility** It is the ability of the person to change direction while moving at or near full speed. More specifically, agility is the ability of a person to change direction or body position quickly (as fast as he can) and regain body control to proceed with another movement.

(*vi*) **Flexibility** In general, flexibility is that quality of the muscles, ligaments and tendons that enables the joints of the body to move easily through a complete range of movement.

(*vii*) **Size of the Muscle** The size of the muscle determines the strength possessed by an individual. Males have bigger and larger muscles due to which they have more strength than females.

(*viii*) **Body Weight** There is a positive correlation between body weight and strength among international weightlifters. So people who weigh heavier are stronger and have more strength than people who are lighter.

(*ix*) **Muscle Composition** Muscles consist of two types of fibres i.e. fast twitch fibres (white fibres) and slow twitch fibres (red fibres).

(*x*) **Intensity of the Nerve Impulse** A muscle consists of many motor units. The number of contracting motor units determines the total force.

(*xi*) **Metabolic Power** The metabolic power depends upon the energy supplied through certain enzymes.

(*xii*) **Aerobic Capacity** The ability of a person to maintain adequate supply of oxygen to the working muscles influences the endurance.

(*xiii*) **Joint Structure** The joint structure of a person determines the range of motions and hence level the flexibility of an individual.

(*xiv*) **Age and Gender** The age of a person as well as the gender determines the level of flexibility. Flexibility decreases with advancement of age and females are more flexible than males.

Effects of Exercise on Cardio-Respiratory System

It has been observed that physical exercises affect the various parameters of the cardio-respiratory system in many ways, which includes both the cardiovascular and respiratory systems.

Effects of exercise on the cardiovascular system are

(*i*) **Cardiac Output** It is the amount of blood pumped by the heart in one minute. In other words, it is the product of stroke volume and heart rate.

Cardiac output increases with the intensity of the exercises. At rest it is 4 to 6 L/min and during exercises it is 20 to 40 L/min.

$$\text{Cardiac output} = \text{heart rate} \times \text{stroke volume}$$
$$= \frac{\text{mL blood}}{\text{min}} \text{ or } \frac{\text{Litres}}{\text{min}}$$

(*ii*) **Heart Rate** The number of cardiac contractions in one minute is called heart rate. Generally normal adult heart rate is 72 beats/min. During exercises the heart rate goes up.

(*iii*) **Stroke Volume** The amount of blood pumped into the aorta with every heartbeat is known as the stroke volume. In an untrained male, it is 70 – 90 mL/beat. In a trained male athlete, it may be 100 – 120 mL/beat. The stroke volume increases in response to the intensity of the exercises.

(*iv*) **Blood Flow** Exercise increases the blood volume caused by a 12% increase in the plasma volume and a slight increase in the red blood cells volume.

With increasing intensities of exercise, a greater accumulation of lactic acid and the production of other metabolic end products (potassium, phosphate) occurs.

This increases blood flow in the cardiac output, while it decreases in the kidneys and abdomen.

Many parameters of respiratory system get affected due to exercises. *Effects of exercise on respiratory system are*

(*i*) **Lung Volume** With endurance training, lung volume and lung capacity increase. Vital capacity, which is maximal volume of air forcefully expelled is increased after endurance training.

(*ii*) **Breathing Frequency** Breathing frequency is the number of breaths per minute. After training, breathing frequency or respiratory rate is decreased.

(*iii*) **Maximum Minute Ventilation** Minute ventilation is the amount of air which is inspired or expired in one minute. After training, maximum, as well as minute ventilation is increased.

(*iv*) **Tidal Volume** Tidal volume, which is the amount of air inspired or expired per breath, is also increased as a result of endurance training.

(*v*) **Ventilatory Efficiency** With physical exercises, particularly endurance training, our ventilatory efficiency increases.

(*vi*) **Pulmonary Diffusion** Pulmonary diffusion is the exchange of gases taking place in the alveoli (small air sacs in our lungs).

Effects of Exercise on the Muscular System

The effects of exercise on the muscular system are as follows

(*i*) **Increase in Blood Flow** The volume of blood flow to muscle tissues increases during exercise. It can increase by upto 25 times during specially demanding exercise.

(*ii*) **Respiration** During exercise, muscles repeatedly contract and relax, using and requiring energy to do so. The energy comes from the chemical ATP that is broken down during exercise into another chemical called ADP. When there is plenty of oxygen available in the muscle tissues, the energy for muscle action is produced aerobically so muscles get more oxygen.

(*iii*) **Muscle Size** Although muscle size (and other physical characteristics such as height) is largely determined by a person's genes but muscle size also gets affected by the intensity of exercises.

(*iv*) **Blood Supply** (to and through muscles) As a result of frequent exercise over a sustained period of time, both the quantity of blood vessels and the extent of the capillary beds increases.

(*v*) **Muscle Coordination** Frequent exercise and specially use of specific muscles for the same or similar skilled tasks.

(*vi*) **Muscle Biochemistry** Many beneficial biochemical changes take place in muscle tissues as a result of regular long–term exercise such as increase in the size and quantity of mitochondria in the cells, increase in the activity of enzymes.

Sports Injuries

Sports injuries are injuries that occur in athletics activities. They can result from acute trauma, or from overuse of a particular body part.

Classification of Sports Injuries

Sports injuries can be classified in various ways. Classification can be based on the time taken for the tissues to become injured, tissue type affected and the severity of the injury.

Several types of injury are as follows

Soft Tissue Injury (STI)

A Soft Tissue Injury (STI) is the damage of muscles, ligaments and tendons throughout the body.

Soft tissue injuries fall into two basic categories

(a) **Acute Injuries** This is one of the most common methods of classifying sports injuries. It is based on the time taken for the tissues to become injured.

(b) **Overuse Injuries** Overuse injuries are not so pervasive and represent a greater challenge for the sports therapist in diagnosis and management.

1. Abrasion

It is a shallow wound, typically a wearing away of the top layer of skin (the epidermis) due to an applied friction force against the body. It may be caused by falling on a hard surface.

The scraped-off surface layer of skin from a abrasion can contain particles of dust or dirt, which may lead to an infection or other complications, if not cleaned and attended properly.

Abrasions are distinguished from **incised wounds**, which are much more serious injuries. While an abrasion is an injury that damages only the superficial layers of skin, incised wound is a deeper cut (typically with a sharp object), that has the potential for serious and severe bleeding.

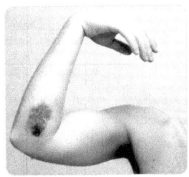

Abrasion

2. Contusion

Contusion is a muscle injury. It can be caused by a direct hit with any sports equipments. It generally happens when an injured capillary or blood vessel leaks blood into the surrounding area.

The raised area of contusion is due to the accumulation of blood and fluid from the injured blood vessels in the tissue.

Stiffness and swelling are common features of contusion. Soft tissue contusions are much easier to diagnose than bone contusions. While both muscle and skin tissue contusions cause pain, muscle tissue contusions are usually more painful, especially if they affect a muscle that you can't avoid using.

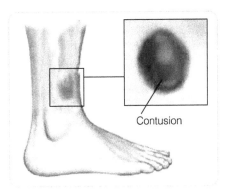

Contusion

3. Laceration

It is basically tearing of the skin that results in an irregular wound. Lacerations may be caused by injury with a sharp object or by impact injury from a blunt object or force.

They may occur anywhere on the body. In most cases, tissue injury is minimal, and infections are uncommon. Severe lacerations are often accompanied by significant bleeding and pain.

Cleaning and preparing a laceration for repair is crucial for preventing infection and reducing the appearance of scarring.

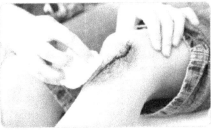

Laceration

4. Incision

An incision wound is a cut in the skin caused by a sharp object such as a knife, broken glass, scissors, etc. However, occasionally these types of wounds can be very deep, cutting into muscle tissue, tendons or major blood vessels. Damage to major blood vessels can cause life-threatening bleeding.

5. Strain

A strain is defined as an injury to a tendon (tissues that connect your muscles and bones) or muscle. Strains often occur in the lower back and the muscle in the back of the thigh.

Some of the symptoms include pain, swelling, muscle spasms and limited ability to move the muscle. Strain can happen as sudden (acute) strain or develop over days (chronic).

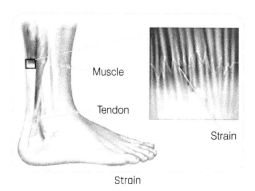

Strain

6. Sprain

A sprain is a stretch or tear of a ligament, a strong band of connective tissue that connects the end of one bone with another. Ligaments stabilise and support the body's joints.

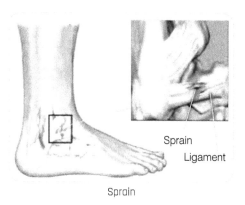

Sprain

Bone and Joint Injuries

The hard tissue injuries take place in bones and cartilages, e.g. a fracture. These injuries are also known as bone and joint injuries. The nature of the damage depends on the direction of the applied force on the bones and the manner in which these bones are attached to other structures.

Bone Injury: Fracture

A hard tissue injury is also called a 'fracture' and is defined as a "loss of continuity in the substance of a bone". In other words, it is a bone injury that breaks the continuity. of bone or seperate it into two or more parts.

Fracture is of various types, which are as follows

1. Greenstick Fracture

A greenstick fracture occurs when a bone bends and cracks, instead of breaking completely into separate pieces. In this type of fracture, arm fractures are most common than leg fractures. It can be caused by many things like participation in sports, motor vehicle accidents and falls.

2. Comminuted Fracture

It is a break or splinter of the bone into more than two fragments.

Since considerable force and energy is required to fragment bone, fractures of this kind occurs after high-impact trauma such as vehicular accidents.

This type of fracture is usually challenging to treat because the break is so complex.

3. Oblique Fracture

An oblique fracture is characterised by a break that is curved or at an diagonal angle to the bone. A sharp blow that comes from an angle (*i.e.* above or below) may cause oblique fractures. They are particularly prone to angulation in the plane of the fracture. Trauma, sudden twist of the muscles or bone diseases may cause oblique fracture.

4. Transverse Fracture

It is a fracture where the bone breaks at a right angle to the long axis of the bone.

Transverse fractures most often occur as the result of strong force applied perpendicular to the long axis of a bone.

This may also be caused due to trauma, sudden twisting of the bone due to muscle spasm or indirect loss of leverage or by certain bone diseases.

5. Impacted Fracture

An impacted fracture is one whose ends of cracked bones are driven into each other. This commonly occurs with arm fractures in children and is sometimes known as a buckle fracture.

In other words, it is a fracture caused when bone fragments are driven into each other. Lifting overweight item is one of the main causing factors of this fracture.

6. Dislocation

Joint injuries typically occur in the knees, ankles, wrists, shoulders and elbows. They can range from sprains to fractures and dislocations.

A **dislocation** is a separation of two bones where they meet at a joint. A dislocated joint is a joint where the bones are no longer in their normal positions.

A dislocated joint may be accompanied by numbness or tingling at the joint or beyond it. It is intensely painful, especially if you try to use joint or put weight on it.

Previous Years'

Examination & Other Important Questions

📄 1 Mark Questions (MCQ)

1. Sprain is an injury of the ....
CBSE 2020

(a) Muscle   (b) Ligament

(c) Joint   (d) Bone

Ans. *(b)* Ligament

2. Laceration is a .... **CBSE 2020**

(a) irregular cut on skin

(b) tissue injury

(c) swelling

(d) ligament injury

Ans. *(a)* irregular cut on skin

3. The capacity of muscles to absorb and consume oxygen is called **CBSE 2020**

(a) Oxygen intake

(b) Oxygen uptake

(c) Oxygen gain

(d) Oxygen transfer

Ans. *(b)* Oxygen uptake

4. The components of physical fitness related to muscles do not include .... of the muscle.

(a) size   (b) strength

(c) endurance   (d) speed

Ans. *(d)* speed

5. Which one of the following is not a component of physical fitness?

(a) Agility

(b) Anaerobic capacity

(c) Flexibility

(d) Muscle composition

Ans. *(b)* Anaerobic capacity

6. The amount of blood pumped by the heart in one minute is known as ....

(a) heart rate   (b) stroke volume

(c) cardiac output   (d) blood flow volume

Ans. *(c)* cardiac output volume

7. In a trained male athlete, the stroke volume normally varies between .... ml/ beat.

(a) 70 and 120   (b) 70 and 90

(c) 90 and 120   (d) 100 and 120

Ans. *(d)* 100 and 120

8. The factor called .... of the respiratory system is decreased after endurance training.

(a) breathing frequency   (b) tidal volume

(c) ventilator efficiency   (d) lung volume

Ans. *(a)* breathing frequency

9. Which of the following is not a beneficial effect on muscle biochemistry due to exercise?

(a) Increase in size and quantity of mitochondria in muscle cells

(b) Better muscle coordination

(c) Increase in the activity of enzymes in the muscles

(d) None of the above

Ans. *(b)* Better muscle coordination

10. Which of the following is bone injury?

(a) Green stick   (b) Oblique

(c) Impacted   (d) All of these

Ans. *(d)* All of these

11. Fractures may be classified as .... and ....

(a) severe, moderate   (b) open, closed

(c) broken, hairline   (d) None of these

Ans. *(b)* open, closed

12. Soft tissue injuries may be classified as .... and ....

(a) mild, acute   (b) acute, overuse

(c) underuse, overuse

(d) hard, special

Ans. *(b)* acute, overuse

13. Which of the following is not a cause of sports injuries?

(a) Equipment selection related

(b) Related to poor technique

(c) Age related causes

(d) None of the above

Ans. *(d)* None of the above

☑ **1 Mark Questions** (VSA)

1. Which type of sports injury is known as 'Strain'? **CBSE 2019**

Ans. The type of sports injury known as 'Strain' is a twist, pull or tearing of a muscle fibre which causes pain, swelling and loss of muscle strength. It is an acute non-contact injury which results due to overstretching or excess contraction of the concerned muscle.

2. What do you mean by soft tissue injuries? **CBSE 2019**

Ans. Soft tissue injuries are damages to any muscles, ligaments or tendons in the body. Common soft tissue injuries usually occur from a sprain, strain, a single blow resulting in a contusion, or overuse of a particular part of the body. Soft tissue injuries can result in pain, swelling, bruising and loss of function.

3. What type of fracture is known as Greenstick fracture? **CBSE 2018**

Ans. Greenstick fracture is a fracture in a young soft bone in which the bone bends and breaks. It is an incomplete break in a bone in which part of the outer shell of the bone remains intact.

4. What is oxygen uptake? **All India 2017**

Ans. Oxygen uptake or VO_2 is the oxygen consumption or uptake per kilogram of body weight. It is a good measure of the respiratory system.

5. What is 'stroke volume'? **All India 2016**

Ans. The amount of blood pumped into the aorta with every heartbeat is known as the stroke volume. In an untrained male, it is 70-90 mL/beat.

6. What kind of sports injury can be termed as abrasion? **All India 2016**

Ans. In dermatology, an abrasion is a wound caused by superficial damage to the skin, no deeper than the epidermis. Mild abrasion is known as grazes or scrapes, a more traumatic abrasion that removes all layers of skin, is known as avulsion.

7. Why does involvement in regular exercise delay the onset of fatigue? **All India 2015**

Ans. Regular exercise delays the onset of fatigue as exercise develops the fitness levels and increases endurance thereby delaying fatigue.

8. Explain the term hypertrophy of muscles. **Delhi 2015**

Ans. Hypertrophy of muscles or muscular hypertrophy is an increase in muscle mass and cross-sectional area. The increase in dimension is due to an increase in the size (not length) of individual muscle fibres.

9. Define physiology.

Ans. Physiology is the study of how the human body functions i.e. how the organs, systems, tissues, cells and molecules work together to maintain our internal environment.

10. Calculate how much blood is pumped by the heart in one minute.

Ans. Blood pumped by the heart in one minute is
Cardiac output = heart rate × stroke volume
$$= 72 \text{ beats/min} \times 70 \text{ mL approximately} = \frac{5040 \text{ mL}}{\text{min}}$$

11. List any four changes happening in the muscular system due to exercising.

Ans. Changes happening in the muscular system due to exercising are
  (i) Change in size and shape of muscle.
  (ii) Increase in the strength of muscles.
  (iii) Increase in coordination.
  (iv) Entrance of greater quantity of oxygen in the body.

12. State the amount of blood pumped in one ventricle beat.

Ans. The amount of blood pumped into the aorta with every heartbeat is known as the stroke volume. In an untrained male, it is 70-90 mL/beat.

13. What is tidal volume?

Ans. Tidal volume is the amount of air inspired or expired per breath. This can be increased with the help of endurance training. In untrained individuals, tidal volume is about 500 mL/breath, whereas in trained persons, it is increased to 600-700 mL/breath.

14. What are acute injuries?

Ans. Acute injuries are the injuries that occur due to sudden trauma to the tissue. The symptoms of acute injuries present themselves almost immediately. For example sprains, fractures, etc.

🔗 3 Marks Questions

1. What are the effects of exercise on muscular system? **CBSE (C) 2018**

Ans. *The effects of exercise on the muscular system are as follows*

(*i*) **Increases Muscle Mass** Through regular exercise, the cells of the muscle are enlarged, which changes the size and shape of the muscles.

(*ii*) **Delays Fatigue** Regular exercise delays fatigue, as fatigue is mainly due to formation of carbon dioxide, lactic acid and acid phosphate in the muscles. The accumulation of these compounds in the muscles is less in a person who performs regular exercise.

(*iii*) **Improves Strength and Speed** Regular exercise improve the strength and speed of the muscle cells. This is partially due to the hypertrophy of the muscles and partially due to increase in the capacity of giving and receiving stimulus.

2. Explain briefly strain and sprain.

Ans. A strain is defined as an injury to a tendon (tissues that connect your muscles and bones) or muscle. Strains often occur in the lower back and the muscle in the back of the thigh.

Some of the symptoms include pain, swelling, muscle spasms and limited ability to move the muscle. Strain can happen as sudden (acute) strain or develop over days (chronic).

A sprain is a stretch or tear of a ligament, a strong band of connective tissue that connects the end of one bone with another. Ligaments stabilise and support the body's joints.

3. How are sports injuries classified?

Ans. Sports injuries are classified in various ways. The classification can be based on the time taken for the tissues to become injured, the tissue type affected and severity of the injury.

These are detailed below

(*i*) Classification based on time taken for the tissue to become injured

    (*a*) Acute injuries

    (*b*) Overuse injuries

(*ii*) Classification based on tissue type affected

    (a) Soft tissue injuries

    (b) Hard tissue injuries

    (c) Special tissue injuries

(*iii*) Classification based on severity

    (*a*) Mild injuries   (*b*) Moderate injuries

    (*c*) Severe injuries

4. What is difference between impacted fracture and greenstick fracture?

Ans. An impacted fracture is one whose ends are driven into each other. This commonly occurs with arm fractures in children and is sometimes known as a buckle fracture.

A greenstick fracture occurs when a bone bends and cracks, instead of breaking completely into separate pieces.

Most greenstick fractures occur in children younger than 10 years of age. This type of broken bone most commonly occur in children.

5. Early morning, we observe many older people following fitness regime. One day Ramu observed a 60-year-old man was holding his chest on the ground. When Ramu approached him, he said that he felt chest pain regularly after jogging.

(i) What is the rate of normal heart beat of an adult?

    (a) 72   (b) 80

    (c) 65   (d) 90

(ii) Age and gender play a very important role in which of these components?

    (a) Endurance

    (b) Strength

    (c) Explosive Strength

    (d) Speed

(iii) Muscular strength starts receding during the age of

    (a) 25-30 years

    (b) 35-40 years

    (c) 45-50 years

    (d) 50-55 years

Ans. (i) - (a),   (ii) - (b),   (iii) - (b)

⎘ 5 Marks Questions

1. Discuss in detail 2 long term and 2 short term effects of exercise on cardio respiratory system. **CBSE Term II 2022**

Ans. There are two main long term effects of exercise on cardio respiratory system

(i) **Stroke Volume** The amount of blood pumped into the aorta with every heartbeat is known as the stroke volume. In an untrained male, it is 70-90 mL/beat. In a trained male athlete, it may be 100 - 120 mL/beat. The stroke volume increases in response to the intensity of the exercises.

(ii) **Blood Flow** Exercise increases the blood volume caused by a 12% increase in the plasma volume and a slight increase in the red blood cells volume. With increasing intensities of exercise, a greater accumulation of lactic acid and the production of other metabolic end products (potassium, phosphate) occurs.

This increases blood flow in the cardiac output, while it decreases in the kidneys and abdomen.

The following given below are the two main short term effects of exercise on cardio respiratory system

(i) **Lung Volume** With endurance training, lung volume and lung capacity increase. Vital capacity, which is maximal volume of air forcefully expelled is increased after endurance training.

(ii) **Pulmonary Diffusion** Pulmonary diffusion is the exchange of gases taking place in the alveoli (small air sacs in our lungs).

2. What are the effects of exercising on the cardiorespiratory system? Explain.
CBSE 2020

Or A trainer can improve the cardiorespiratory system with the help of exercise. Justify this statement.

Ans. The cardiorespiratory system consists of organs responsible for taking in oxygen for respiration and releasing carbon dioxide and water vapour, which are the waste products formed during respiration. The passages in the nose, windpipe (trachea), bronchi, lungs and air sacs are the main organs of the respiratory system.

A trainer can improve the cardiorespiratory system with the help of exercise by

(i) **Decrease in Rate of Respiration** When a beginner starts exercise, then his rate of respiration increases. But when the same individual performs exercise daily, then his rate of respiration decreases in comparison to the beginning stage at rest.

(ii) **Lung Volume** For normal breathing at rest, lung expand and there is a change in air pressure. During exercise, due to rapid movement of diaphragm and intercostal muscles, total area of lung expands to accommodate more exchange of gases.

(iii) **Lung Diffusion Capacity** During exercise, the lung diffusion capacity increases in both trained and untrained persons.

However, trained athletes may increase their diffusion capacity 30% more than that of an untrained person because athlete's lung surface area and red blood cell count is higher than that of non-athletes.

(iv) **Pulmonary Ventilation** The amount of air passing through lungs each minute is called Pulmonary Ventilation.

The Pulmonary Ventilation (PV) is a producet of Tidal Volume (TV and Respiratory Rate (RR) and therefore at rest it is around 8 l/min.

During exercise time both TV and RR increase, due to which PV will also increase depending on the intensity of exercise.

For an ordinary person, the value of PV may be 40-50 l/min and for well trained athlete, it may be around 100 l/min.

(v) **Residual Air Volume** It is the volume of air in the lungs which is left after exhalation. With exercises, the residual air capacity increases which enhances efficiency of lungs.

3. What do you understand by fracture? How can fractures be classified? Explain.
CBSE 2019

Ans. A fracture is a break in the continuity of a bone or a separation of a bone into two or more parts. It occurs when a force exerted against a bone is stronger than the bone can bear.

This disturbs the structure and strength of the bone and leads to pain, loss of function, soft tissue damage, sometimes bleeding and injury around the site. Some common bone fractures are knee fracture, wrist fracture, collar bone fracture, ankle bone fracture etc.

Fractures are of different types. Some of them are discussed below

(*i*) **Green Stick Fracture** It is a fracture in a young soft bone in which the bone bends and breaks. It is an incomplete break in a bone in which part of the outer-shell of the bone remains intact. This type of fractures occur usually in young boys as their bones are soft and not properly developed.

(*ii*) **Comminuted Fracture** A comminuted fracture happens when the bone involved is actually broken into several pieces. This type of fracture is usually challenging to treat because the break is so complex. It typically occurs with elderly people or with people involved in accidents, or people with conditions which weaken the bone, such as osteoporosis or cancer.

(*iii*) **Transverse Fracture** It is a type of fracture in which the fracture occurs across the bone at a right angle to the longitudinal axis of the bone. This may be caused due to trauma, sudden twisting of the bone due to muscle spasm or indirect loss of leverage or by certain bone diseases.

(*iv*) **Oblique Fracture** It is a type of fracture in which the fracture occurs across the bone in a diagonal way, instead of break at right angles or parallel to the axis of the bone. Trauma, sudden twist of the muscles or bone diseases may cause oblique fracture.

(*v*) **Impacted Fracture** This is a fracture in which the ends of the cracked bones are driven into each other. It is a loss in continuity in the structure of bones i.e. breaks or cracks, in which at least one bone (or fragment of bone) has been driven into another.

4. Write in detail about the dislocation and fractures among the bones and joint injuries. **All India 2016**

Ans. The musculoskeletal system comprises over half the body mass. The most common musculoskeletal dysfunctions are joint stiffness, joint swelling and joint pains.

Bones, being non-yielding structures, are damaged when excessive force is applied directly or indirectly. The nature of the damage depends on the direction of the applied force on the bones and the manner in which these bones are attached to other structures.

The principal acute skeletal injuries are sprains, strains, subluxation, fractures and dislocations.

Many fractures and dislocation complications such as nerve and vessel injury occur not from the trauma itself but from poor first-aid which does not provide adequate splinting prior to movement. Traumatic bone injury rarely occurs without significant soft-tissue damage. Fractures are classified as open and closed.

An open fracture is one in which there is a break in the skin that is contiguous with the fracture. The bone is either protruding from the wound or exposed through a channel, which can be produced by an arrow, javelin, bullet or other ways.

5. What are the various factors affecting physiological fitness? Explain. **All India 2015**

or Describe physiological factors determining components of physical fitness.

Ans. *Physiological factors determining components of physical fitness are*

(*i*) **Muscular Strength** This is the maximum force or tension a muscle or a muscle group can exert against a resistance. Physiologically the muscle will increase in strength only if it has to increase its workload beyond what is ordinarily required of it.

(*ii*) **Power** This is the ability of the body to release maximum muscle contraction in the shortest possible time.

(*iii*) **Speed** This is the rapidity with which one can repeat successive movements of the same pattern.

(*iv*) **Muscular Endurance** This is the ability of a muscle or muscle group to perform repeated contractions against a resistance / load or to sustain contraction for an extended period of time with less discomfort and more rapid recovery.

(*v*) **Agility** This is the ability of a person to change direction or body position as quickly as possible and regain body control to proceed with another movement.

(*vi*) **Flexibility** This is a quality of the muscles, ligaments and tendons that enables the joints of the body to move easily through a complete range of movements.

6. Recall the adaptive effects that take place in our body after engaging in exercise for a longer period.

Ans. The adaptive effects that take place in body after engaging in exercise for a longer period are

(*i*) **Increase in Heart Size** We cannot do the exercise on our heart directly, but when we perform any exercise regularly, our heart size increases. Exercising develops the muscles of the heart.

(*ii*) **Increase in Heart Rate** Generally an adult has a heart rate of 72 beats per minute while resting, but when he exercises, his heart rate increases as per the intensity and duration of the exercise.

(*iii*) **Increase in Stroke Volume** Stroke volume is the quantity of blood which the heart pumps out in a single stroke. Due to the heart's size increasing, the stroke volume increases.

(*iv*) **Decrease in Cholesterol Level** Regular exercise reduces the cholesterol level in our blood, which has a direct link with the blood pressure.

(*v*) **Increase in Number and Efficiency of Capillaries** Regular exercise increases the number of capillaries and their efficiency.

(*vi*) **Reduced Risk of Heart Diseases** Regular exercise gradually reduces stress related hormones from circulating in the blood. This results in increase of blood flow in the blood vessels, which in turn, lowers the risk of building up of plaque which affects the heart. Hence, regular exercise reduces the risk of heart diseases.

7. A trainer can improve the respiratory system with the help of exercise. Justify this statement.

Ans. The respiration system consists of organs responsible for taking in oxygen for respiration and releasing carbon dioxide and water vapour, which are the waste products formed during respiration. The passages in the nose, windpipe (trachea), bronchi, lungs and air sacs are the main organs of the respiratory system.

A trainer can improve the respiratory system with the help of exercise by

(*i*) **Increasing the Lung Volume and Capacity** Vital capacity, which is the maximal volume of air forcefully expired after a maximal inspiration, in a normal untrained person may be 3-4 litres, but in a trained athlete this goes upto 5-6 litres.

(*ii*) **Reducing the Breathing Frequency** In a normal untrained individual, the resting breathing frequency is about 12-20 breaths/min, whereas in trained athletes, it comes down to 7-8 breaths/min.

(*iii*) **Maximising the Minute Ventilation** Maximum minute ventilation in an untrained individual is about 100 L/min, whereas in trained athletes it increases to more than 150-160 L/min.

(*iv*) **Increasing the Tidal Volume** In an untrained individual, tidal volume is about 500 mL/breath, whereas in trained persons, it increases to more than 600-700 mL/breath.

(*v*) **Increasing the Ventilatory Efficiency** Normally, 15 L of air is required to get 1 L of oxygen but a trained individual gets the same amount of oxygen, i.e. one litre, from less air i.e. 12 L.

(*vi*) **Increasing the Pulmonary Diffusion** During maximal level of exercise, more alveoli become active for diffusion. The size of the alveoli is also increased, which provides more space for diffusion of gases such as oxygen (O_2) and carbon dioxide (CO_2).

CHAPTER 08

Biomechanics and Sports

Biomechanics is the branch of Kinesiology which deals with the precise information of human movements using scientific methods. It is the application of mechanical principles in the study of living organisms so as to prevent injuries and train physical movements.

Newton's Laws of Motion and their Application in Sports

Laws of Motion

Sir Issac Newton made three laws of motion which are explained below

(*i*) **Newton's First Law of Motion** This law is also known as law of inertia. This law states that a body at rest will remain at rest and a body in motion will remain in motion at the same speed and in the same direction till any external force is applied on it to change that state.

(*ii*) **Newton's Second Law of Motion** This law states that the rate of change of momentum of an object is directly proportional to the force producing it.

$$a = \frac{F}{m} \quad \text{where} \quad a \propto F, \ a \propto \frac{1}{m}$$

(*iii*) **Newton's Third Law of Motion** This law states that to every action, there is always an equal and opposite reaction. This law describes what happens to a body when it exerts a force on another body. These three laws are still being used to this day to describe the kinds of objects and speeds that we encounter in everyday life.

Application of Laws of Motion in Sports

First Law

(*i*) **Softball** The ball is hit into the air. Eventually, gravity will act on the ball, pulling it down to the ground. Then, it will roll until friction between the ball and the grass stops it.

(*ii*) **Soccer** When a soccer ball is kicked into the air, gravity will pull it back to the ground. Then, it will continue to roll until friction between the ball and the grass slows it down.

(*iii*) **Dance** When a dancer leaps, he/she only stays in the air for a short amount of time because air resistance and gravity works against them.

(*iv*) **Basketball** When a basketball is shot, it takes a parabolic path due to gravity acting on it. Then it slows down due to air resistance and fluid friction.

Second Law

If a baseball player hits a ball with double the force, the rate at which the ball will accelerate (speed up) will be doubled. Football players can slow down, stop or reverse the direction of other players depending upon how much force they can generate and in which direction.

Third Law

A swimmer propels herself through the water because the water offers enough counterforce to oppose the action of her hands pushing, allowing her to move. An athlete can jump higher off a solid surface because it opposes his body with as much force as he is able to generate, in contrast to sand or other unstable surface.

Equilibrium

Equilibrium can be defined as a state of balance among forces acting within or upon a body. In other words, it is a state in which all influences, forces are cancelled or counterbalanced by each other *i.e.* the sum of all opposite forces acting on it is zero. Thus, it is a scientific term describing balance and stability.

In the human body, a state of equilibrium occurs when its centre of gravity lies over the base and the gravity line falls within the base of the body.

The greater the body surface in contact with the ground, the larger is the base of support. Hence, the posture of sitting is more stable, easier and more comfortable than the posture of standing.

There are two types of equilibrium

1. **Dynamic Equilibrium**

It is a state of balance of all applied forces acting on a moving body.
In simple words, when the moving body is stable and balanced such that it results in movement with unchanging speed and direction, then the body is said to be in dynamic equilibrium.
For instance, when a sportsperson is running, or taking part in gymnastics.

2. **Static Equilibrium** It is a state of balance that occurs when the body is at rest or in a motionless position, *i.e.* when the centre of gravity is in a static position.

For instance, standing on one leg, sitting on a chair, etc.

Centre of Gravity

The balance and stability of an individual depends upon the centre of gravity. Centre of gravity of a body is an imaginary point around which the body of the object is balanced. In human being, the centre of gravity can simply be considered as the centre of weight of the body.

The weight of the body is just the sum of individual weights of its components like arms, legs etc. The centre of gravity has the property of continuously changing during movement. The centre of gravity depends on the shape and size of the body. If a body has more mass distributed in its upper part, the centre of gravity will be towards the top of the body. Centre of gravity always changes its direction according to movement.

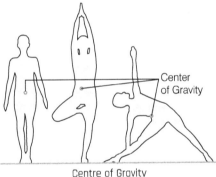

Centre of Gravity

For instance, a basketball player, while jumping up to score a basket, swings both arms upward and forward to raise his centre of gravity and thus reach the maximum height. But once in the air, the player drops one arm to his side and tries to reach the maximum with the other arm to score a basket. This reduces his centre of gravity, so that he does not become unstable.

Applications of Centre of Gravity in Sports

The knowledge of equilibrium and centre of gravity are essential for sports and physical education. The ability of balance whether in stationary position or in movement, is a key to success in most of sports and physical activities.

Proper application of the concepts in sports can improve performance. This can be done by following the methods given below

- A sportsperson can become more stable by lowering his/her centre of gravity.
- To maintain balance during a performance, the sports person must ensure that the centre of gravity remains over and nearer his support base. When the center of gravity is beyond the base, balance is lost.
- For rapid movement of his body from a position of readiness, the sportsperson should position his body so that his centre of gravity has to move the minimum distance to clear the support base. This is particularly applicable during the start of sprint races.
- Shifting the centre of gravity towards an approaching force increases the sportsperson's ability to maintain balance.

When lifting or carrying an object, shift the body weight in order to maintain balance.

Friction and Sports

The force acting along two surfaces in contact which opposes the motion of one body over the other is called the force of friction.

Friction is of two types

(*i*) **Static Friction** The opposing force that comes into play when one body tends to move over the another surface but the actual motion has yet not started is called static friction.

(*ii*) **Dynamic Friction** It is the friction between two surfaces that are in relative motion with respect to each other. It is the opposing force that comes into play when one body is actually moving over the surface of another body.

Methods of Reducing Friction

(*i*) **Polishing** By polishing the surfaces in contact, they become smooth and the force of friction reduces. Many implements like the discus are painted to reduce friction.

(*ii*) **Lubrication** The lubrication of surfaces makes them slippery and this reduces the force of friction.

(*iii*) **Streamlining** Friction due to air is reduced by streamlining the shape of the body. The aeroplanes are made with a sharp front to reduce friction.

(*iv*) **Use of Ball Bearings** Ball bearings are used to reduce the force of friction.

Many sports require more friction and other need lesser friction. For instance, in athletics, the shoes are designed to increase friction so that better speed can be generated. This is accomplished by fixing spikes on the bottom of the athletes' shoes.

Friction in Sports

It is important to understand the role of friction in sports to bring efficiency in playing that sport. Friction is also called a necessary evil. It may hamper performance in certain sports like cycling, roller skating, skiing etc.

If the friction is more, then the cyclist will have to put more effort to cycle. If there is less friction between the road and tyres, then it will become too slippery and the cyclist may fall. Athletes, footballers, hockey players and sprinters, prefer to wear studs (shoes with spikes) to have proper friction that helps them in running fast without slipping.

Likewise, sportsperson performing various sports like weightlifting and gymnastics like to pad their palms with lime powder for better grip of the horizontal bars. Badminton, squash players who need to hold the racket firmly also use gripping tapes to manage friction.

Projectile in Sports

A projectile is anything which is thrown or jumped into the air. Once it has left the ground it will follow a flight path called a parabola until it once mor,e comes back down to earth. This applies to balls, javelins, discus, long jumpers, high jumpers, and horses show jumping.

An object must be dropped from a height, thrown vertically upwards or thrown at an angle to be considered a projectile. The path followed by a projectile is known as a trajectory.

If gravity were not present, a projectile would travel in a constant straight line. However, the presence of gravity forces projectiles to travel in a parabolic trajectory, thus gravity accelerates objects downwards.

Factors Affecting the Trajectory

Factors affecting the trajectory are as follows

- Angle of projection
- Projection velocity
- Relative height of projection

In order to analyse projectile motion, it is divided into two components, horizontal motion and vertical motion. Perpendicular components of motion are independent of each other i.e. the horizontal and vertical motions of a projectile are independent. Horizontal motion of an object has no external forces acting upon it (with the exception of air resistance but this is generally not accounted for).

Due to this absence of horizontal forces, a projectile remains in motion with a constant horizontal velocity, covering equal distances over equal periods in time. Thus no horizontal acceleration is occurring. The degree of vertical velocity however, is reduced by the effect of gravity.

Force of gravity acts on the initial vertical velocity of the javelin, reducing the velocity until it equals zero. A vertical velocity of zero represents the apex of the trajectory, meaning that the projectile has reached its max height. During the downward flight of the projectile, vertical velocity increases due to the effect of gravity.

Previous Years'

Examination & Other Important Questions

☑ 1 Mark Questions (MCQ)

1. "Acceleration of an object is directly proportional to the force exerted upon it." It is related with **CBSE Term I 2021**
   (a) Newton's Ist Law of Motion
   (b) Newton's IInd Law of Motion
   (c) Newton's IIIrd Law of Motion
   (d) Both (a) and (b)

Ans. (b) Newton's IInd Law of Motion

2. Newton's which law states that every object will remain at rest or in motion until any external force is applied? **CBSE Term I 2021**
   (a) Newton's Ist Law of motion
   (b) Newton's IInd Law of motion
   (c) Newton's IIIrd Law of motion
   (d) Both (a) and (b)

Ans (a) Newton's Ist Law of motion

3. Friction always acts .... the motion of an object. **CBSE 2020**
   (a) in the same direction as
   (b) perpendicular to
   (c) opposite to
   (d) at a 45 degree angle to

Ans (c) opposite to

4. Which of the following Newton's laws of motion applies to an athlete performing a high jump off a solid surface?
   (a) First
   (b) Second
   (c) Third
   (d) All of these

Ans. (c) Third

5. A basketball shot towards the basket follows a parabolic path due to ....
   (a) friction with the air
   (b) effect of Newton's third law of motion
   (c) gravitation
   (d) All of the above

Ans. (c) gravitation

6. The force of friction .... the motion of one body over the other.
   (a) opposes
   (b) supports
   (c) helps
   (d) does not affect

Ans. (a) opposes

7. Static friction comes into play when ....
   (a) two bodies are in contact and force is applied to one of them
   (b) two bodies are in contact and the same force is applied to both of them
   (c) two bodies are not in contact and force is applied to one of them
   (d) two bodies are not in contact and the same force is applied to both of them

Ans. (a) two bodies are in contact and force is applied to one of them

8. Dynamic friction is the force opposing motion of one body over the surface of another body when ....
   (a) the bodies are not in contact with each other
   (b) the bodies have not yet started moving
   (c) one body is actually moving
   (d) None of the above

Ans. (c) one body is actually moving

9. Sliding friction is a form of dynamic friction applicable in the sport/ sporting event of
   (a) running sprints
   (b) broad jump
   (c) tennis
   (d) ice skating

Ans. (d) ice skating

10. Rolling friction is a form of dynamic friction applicable in the sport of ....
   (a) cricket   (b) hockey
   (c) football   (d) All of these
Ans. (d) All of these

11. In which of the following sports is friction beneficial for performance?
   (a) Cycling   (b) Football
   (c) Both (a) and (b) (d) Neither (a) nor (b)
Ans. (b) Football

12. .... the bottom surface of an athlete's shoes increases friction between the shoes and the ground.
   (a) Putting spikes on (b) Polishing
   (c) Streamlining   (d) None of these
Ans. (a) Putting spikes on

13. Friction may be reduced by ....
   (a) roughening   (b) lubrication
   (c) smoothening   (d) All of these
Ans. (b) lubrication

14. Badminton players rub the soles of their shoes with lime so as to ....
   (a) reduce friction between their feet and the court
   (b) increase friction between their feet and the court
   (c) enable them to run faster on court
   (d) None of the above
Ans. (b) increase friction between their feet and the court

15. Rishi who was studying in class XII is a science stream student. During his Physical Education class, he got confused how Newton's Laws of Motion are useful in sports and how they can be applied in sports. But his teacher explained these laws with help of examples from sports which proved to be very helpful for him Swimming is the best example of which law of motion?
   (a) Law of Inertia
   (b) Law of Acceleration
   (c) Law of Reaction
   (d) Both (a) and (c)
Ans. (c) Law of Reaction

16. Assertion (A) "A change in the acceleration of an object is directly proportional to the force producing it and inversely proportional to its mass."

   Reason (R) Lighter mass will travel at a faster speed.

   Codes
   (a) Both A and R are true and R is the correct explanation of A
   (b) Both A and R are true, but R is not the correct explanation of A
   (c) A is true, but R is false
   (d) A is false, but R is true
Ans. (b) Both A and R are true and R is the correct explanation of A

🗹 1 Mark Questions (VSA)

1. Explain what is 'dynamic friction'.
   All India 2016
Ans. Dynamic friction is the opposing force that comes into play when one body is actually moving over the surface of another body. Dynamic friction may be of two types, i.e. sliding friction and rolling friction.

2. What is Newton's first law of motion?
Ans. This law states that a body at rest will remain at rest and a body in motion will remain in motion at the same speed and in the same direction till any external force is applied on it to change state.

3. Enlist the methods of reducing friction.
Ans. Methods of reducing friction are
   (*i*) Polishing
   (*ii*) Lubrication
   (*iii*) Use of ball bearings
   (*iv*) Streamlining

4. What is Equilibrium?
Ans. Equilibrium can be defined as a state of balance among forces acting within or upon a body.

5. What do you understand by the term static equilibrium?
Ans. When the forces that act upon an object are equally blanced and its centre of gravity is in a static position , the object is consider to be in a state of static equilibrium.

☑ 3 Marks Questions

1. How can Newton's second law and third law of motion be applied in sports?

Ans. **Second Law** If a baseball player hits a ball with double the force, the rate at which the ball will accelerate (speed up) will be doubled. Football players can slow down, stop, or reverse their direction depending upon how much force they can generate and in which direction.

Third Law A swimmer propels herself through the water because the water offers enough counter force to oppose the action of her hands pushing, allowing her to move. An athlete can jump higher off a solid surface because it opposes his body with as much force as he is able to generate, in contrast to sand or other unstable surface.

2. "Friction is a necessary evil." Justify your answer with suitable examples from sport.

Ans. Friction is usually called a necessary evil. It means that it is essential in games and sports. Without friction, we cannot give a better performance in the field of sports.

Examples are spikes used by athletes for running and studs used in football boots of the players. However, friction has disadvantages also. In cycling, there should not be more friction between road and the tyres of the cycle.

3. Explain what is Dynamic Equilibrium?

Ans. It is a state of balance of all applied forces acting on a moving body.

In simple words, when the moving body is stable and balanced such that it results in movement with unchanging speed and direction, then the body is said to be in dynamic equilibrium.

4. Explain about centre of gravity?

Ans. The balance and stability of an individual depends upon the centre of gravity. Centre of gravity of a body is an imaginary point around which the body of the object is balanced. In human being, the centre of gravity can simply be considered as the centre of weight of the body.

5. What is projectile in sorts?

Ans. A projectile is anything which is thrown or jumped into the air. Once it has left the ground it will follow a flight path called a parabola until it once more comes back down to earth. This applies to balls, javelins, discus, long jumpers, high jumpers, and horses show jumping.

☑ 5 Marks Questions

1. Explain Newton's laws of Motion and their application in sports. **CBSE 2020**

Or With the help of suitable examples discuss the application of Newton's Laws of Motion in sports. **CBSE (C) 2018**

Ans. All of Newton's laws of motion have application in sports. *Each law and its application in sports is discussed below*

- **Newton's First Law** states that a body at rest will remain at rest and a body in motion will remain in motion at the same speed and in the same direction till any external force is applied on it to change that state. This has application in a game such as soccer as, when a soccer ball is kicked along the ground, it will continue to roll until the frictional force of the ground on the ball ultimately brings it to a stop.

- **Newton's Second Law** states that the acceleration of an object is directly proportional to the force producing it and inversely proportional to its mass. This has application in a game such as baseball in which, if a batter hits the ball with double the normal force, the acceleration of the ball will be doubled.

- **Newton's Third Law** states that, to every action, there is always an equal and opposite reaction. This has application in a sport such as swimming, in which a swimmer propels himself through the water because the water offers an equal counterforce to oppose the action of the swimmer's hands and legs, thus allowing him to move.

2. What is friction? Is it advantageous and disadvantageous in the field of games and sports? **All India 2017**

Ans. Friction is the force acting along two surfaces in contact which opposes the motion of one body over the other. It has very importance in sports. For example, when a cricket ball or hockey ball is hit, it moves very fast in the direction of force in the ground. After sometimes its motion becomes less and ultimately it comes in static position.

Advantages

Friction has a great significance in the field of sports. Many sports require more friction and other need lesser friction. In some sports we can not give a better performance without friction.

For example, in athletics, the shoes are designed to increase friction so that better speed can be generated.

The spikes have small nails to crease the friction. Gymnasts sometimes use lime on their palms to perform on horizontal bar, uneven bars to increase friction. In these sports friction is necessary thus regarded as advantageous.

Disadvantages

On the other hand, some games do not require friction. For example, the games like snow skiing, the skiis are designed to have minimum friction. In cycling there should not be more friction between road and tyres of the cycle. Thus the tyre should be fully inflated to reduce the force of friction. If there is more friction, it will be more wastage of energy of the cyclist. Moreover, the cyclists use pointed helmets, silk body fitted costume and bend their bodies while cycling to reduce air friction. Swimmers use goggles, cap and full body swimsuit to reduce the force of friction caused by water. In roller skating, less friction is also needed for better performance. Thus in these games friction is regarded as disadvantageous.

3. Elucidate the types of friction.

Ans. The force acting along two surfaces in cozntact which opposes the motion of one body over the other is called the force of friction. It is very important in sports. The larger the area of contact between the surfaces, the greater is the force of friction. When both the surfaces are smooth, the force of friction reduces to almost zero.

Two types of friction are

   (*i*) **Static Friction** The opposing force that comes into play when one body tends to move over the another surface but the actual motion has not yet started.

   (*ii*) **Dynamic Friction** It is the friction between two surfaces that are in relative motion with respect to each other. It is the opposing force that comes into play when one body is actually moving over the surface of another body. Dynamic friction may be of two types, i.e. sliding friction and rolling friction.

4. The teachers as well as coaches always make their best efforts to improve the performance of their students in various competitive games and sports.

They can help to improve the performance of students if they have adequate knowledge of biomechanics. **CBSE QB 2021**

   (i) The more force one exerts on the downward bounce, the higher the ball bounces into the air. Which law is this statement being referred to?
   (a) Newton's 1st law
   (b) Newton's 2nd law
   (c) Newton's 3rd law
   (d) Law of gravitation

  (ii) Among the above given pictures, Newton's 3rd law is depicted in
   (a) First   (b) Second
   (c) Both (a) and (b)(d) None of these

 (iv) The study of human body and various forces acting on it is
   (a) Biology   (b) Biomechanics
   (c) Physiology   (d) Anatomy

  (v) A high jumper can jump higher off a solid surface because it opposes his or her body with as much force as he or she is able to generate. This example refers to
   (a) Law of conservation
   (b) Law of inertia
   (c) Law of action and reaction
   (d) Law of gravity

Ans. (i) - (c),   (ii) - (c),   (iii) - (b),   (iv) - (b),   (v) - (c)

CHAPTER 09

Psychology and Sports

Personality

The word personality is derived from the Latin word *persona* meaning *the mask*. In ancient Greece, the actors used to wear masks to hide their identities while portraying their roles in a theatrical play. To an ordinary person, the word personality conveys the meaning of one's physical appearance, habits, ways of dressing, reputation, manners and other similar characteristics.

Definitions of Personality

According to Macionis, "It is the constant pattern of thinking, feeling and actions."

According to Ogburn and Nimkoff, "The totality of sentiments, attitudes, ideas, habits, skills and behaviours of an individual is personality."

Types of Personality

The concept of personality and its types have been formulated by many psychologists.

Personality Types According to Jung

Carl Jung distinguished people according to the nature and attitude of the person. *They are as follows*

1. **Extroverts-Introverts** This represents a person's direction of energy expression. An extrovert is more open as the direction of energy is derived and expressed in the external world, environment and surroundings. On the other hand, an introvert is mainly confined to internal world.

2. **Sensing-Intuition** This represents the way by which a person perceives information. Sensing means that the person perceives information that he receives through the senses or external world. On the other hand, intuition (natural instinct) means that the person believes mainly information that he receives through the inner-self or imaginary world.

3. **Thinking-Feeling** This represents the way a person processes information. Thinking means a person processes or makes a decision by logical reasoning.

   On the other hand, feeling means that a person processes information based on emotions.

4. **Judging-Perceiving** This represents the way how a person implements the information that has been processed. Judging means moving in a systematic manner by organising the life's events according to the plans made.

   On the other hand, perceiving means exploring alternative options or moving spontaneously at times without much planning.

Personality Traits (Big Five Theory)

The 'big five' are the broad categories of five personality traits that are universal. *They are as follows*

- **Extraversion** It is characterised by excitability, sociability, talkativeness, assertiveness and high amounts of emotional expressiveness. People high in extraversion are extroverts and low in extraversion are introverts.
- **Agreeableness** This includes attributes like trust, kindness, affection and other social behaviours. People high in agreeableness are more cooperative and people low in this trait are more competitive and manipulative.
- **Conscientiousness** Characteristics include high level of thoughtfulness, good impulse control and goal-directed behaviours. People high on this trait are organised and mindful of details.
- **Neuroticism** Characteristics are sadness, moodiness and emotional instability. People high in this trait experience mood swings, anxiety, irritability and sadness. People low in this trait are more stable and emotionally resilient.
- **Openness** Characteristics are imagination and insight. People high in this trait are creative, adventurous and have a broad range of interests. People low in this trait are more traditional and less in abstract thinking.

Aggression in Sports

Aggression or aggressiveness means the intention to cause mental or physical harm to a person. This is done by doing physical harm, showing unkind or nasty behaviour, abusing or using cruel words.

A person shows aggression due to stress, anger or even due to insecurity. Aggression may come instantly or may build up over time. It can be positive as well as negative.

According to **Baron and Richardsons**, "Any form of behaviour towards the goal of harming or injuring another living being who is motivated to avoid such treatment is aggression."

Concept of Aggression in Sports

In sports, aggression is often seen in the field where players play aggressively. There is a desire to excel which leads the players to play with high intensity. So aggression is positive when players play within the rules of the game with high intensity and without harming other players.

However aggression becomes negative when players have an intention to harm other players, use abusive language or doing other such things which are not within the laws of the game. For example, pushing another player over a game of football or using abusive language for other players or teams.

Types of Aggression in Sports

In sports, aggression has been defined into two kinds or types. These are instrumental aggression and hostile aggression.

1. **Instrumental Aggression** In instrumental aggression, the main aim is to achieve a goal by using aggression. It is a positive form of aggression. Here the aim of the player is to excel in the sport that he is playing through high intensity output and competitive spirit.

   For example, a football player using aggression to tackle his opponent and win the ball. He is not harming any player but only using his aggressiveness to gain the ball. Experienced players show instrumental aggression on the field as they have greater self-control to manage their aggression.

2. **Hostile Aggression** In hostile aggression, the main aim is to cause harm or injury to your opponent. It is usually an unplanned, impulsive reaction towards a player who may have become a threat in achieving the goal. However it may also be planned to cause injury to intended player on the field. This kind of aggression often arises from insult, hurt, bad feelings, jealousy and threat.

   For example, a bowler throwing a bouncer to deliberately injure the batsman or to shake up his concentration. In some extreme cases, hitting an opponent or deliberately obstructing his path leads to his fall on the ground.

This kind of aggression is usually seen in new players who want to achieve success quickly.

The difference between the two is that instrumental aggression is positive where the aim is to excel by own efforts while hostile aggression is negative. Here the aim is to excel by causing harm to others.

Psychological Attributes in Sports

Sometimes the mental aspect of sports is just as important as the physical aspect. Studies have shown that athletes who dream about their success, talk to themselves, and imagine success in their brains will perform better on the field.

Psychological attributes such as self-esteem, mental imagery, goal setting, self-talk, and others have been empirically shown to help an athlete succeed.

Self-Esteem

In psychology, the term self-esteem is used to describe a person's overall subjective sense of personal worth. In other words, self-esteem may be defined as how much you appreciate and like yourself regardless of the circumstances.

Self-esteem impacts our decision-making process, relationships, emotional health, and our overall well-being. It also influences motivation, as sportspersons with a healthy, positive view of themselves understand their potential and may feel inspired to take on new challenges in sports.

Mental Imagery

Mental imagery involves the athlete imagining themselves in an environment performing a specific activity using their senses (sight, hear, feel and smell).

Mental Imagery itself can be useful in several circumstances, including:

- Developing self-confidence.

- Developing pre-competition and competition strategies which teach athletes to cope with new situations before they encounter them.
- Helping the athlete to focus his/her attention or concentrate on a particular skill he/she is trying to learn or develop.
- The competition situation.

Self- Talk

Self-talk is defined as the verbalisation or statements athletes repeat to themselves prior to or during skill execution. Performing these techniques can improve focus and slow the brain down, giving it the ability to devote more power to the specific task at hand.

The goal of self-talk is to replace negative thinking with more positive messages.

For instance, a basketball player preparing to shoot free throws should never tell him or herself, "I'm not going to make this shot." If they do, they need to consider how self-talk can help them.

Goal Setting

Goal setting is a mental training technique to increase motivation and enhance confidence. It is used widely across all levels of sport, and goals provide essential direction at both an immediate and long-term level. These goals can be broken down into three categories

- (*i*) **Outcome goals** which deals with specific results in competition.
- (*ii*) **Performance goals** which deals with helping an athlete make improvements over a period of time.
- (*iii*) **Process goals** which are the aspects a competitor should be concentrating on when carrying out a specific skill.

Goal setting helps to focus attention and it is critical to maintain and enhance motivation. Goal setting gives direction both in the short term and the long term and you can see success as you achieve your short term goals."

Previous Years'

Examination & Other Important Questions

☑ 1 Mark Questions (MCQ)

1. Traits like insight, imagination, receptivity towards new ideas are involved with **CBSE 2020**
(a) Openness
(b) Conscientiousness
(c) Agreeableness
(d) Extroversion

Ans. (a) Openness

2. To an ordinary person, personality does not include one's ....
(a) manner of dressing
(b) method of solving problems
(c) physical appearance
(d) reputation

Ans. (b) method of solving problems

3. Carl Jung classified personalities on the basis of ....
(a) physical attributes
(b) traits
(c) mentality
(d) None of the above

Ans. (c) mentality

4. Extroverts are ....
(a) very social
(b) outgoing and lively
(c) full of self-confidence
(d) All of the above

Ans. (d) All of the above

5. Jung classified most of the people as ....
(a) ambiverts
(b) mesomorphs
(c) extroverts
(d) introverts

Ans. (a) ambiverts

6. Which of the following is a personality trait not included in the 'big five'?
(a) Neuroticism
(b) Extraversion
(c) Aggressiveness
(d) Agreeableness

Ans. (c) Aggressiveness

7. Which of the following qualities is characteristic of openness as a personality trait?
(a) Emotionally unstable
(b) Having goal-directed behaviour
(c) Emotionally expressive
(d) Having a broad range of interests

Ans. (d) Having a broad range of interests

8. Aggression is displayed in sports through
(a) unsportsmanlike behaviour
(b) use of abusive words
(c) physically attacking another participant due to anger
(d) All of the above

Ans. (d) All of the above

9. In instrumental aggression, the main aim is to .... using aggression.
(a) cause harm to the opponent
(b) achieve a positive goal
(c) express your feeling of jealousy
(d) show your hostility to an opponent

Ans. (b) achieve a positive goal

☑ 1 Mark Questions (VSA)

1. Define personality.

Ans. According to Ogburn and Nimkoff, "The totality of sentiments, attitude, idea, habits, skills and behaviours of an individual is personality."

2. What do you understand by aggression in sports?

Ans. In sports, aggression means the desire to harm another player which is not within the laws of the game. For example, pushing another player over a game in football or using abusive language for other players or teams.

3. What is the aim of hostile aggression?

Ans. The main aim is to cause harm or injury to the opponent. It is usually unplanned, impulsive reaction. For example, a bowler throwing a bouncer to deliberately injure the batsman.

4. What do you mean by the term sports psychology?

Ans. Sports psychology is that branch of psychology which refers to the study of human behaviour on the playfield, both under-practice and competitive situations, with a view to bring about qualitative improvement in performance and maintain the same even during the stress of competition.

5. What is Mental imagery?

Ans. Mental imagery involves the athlete imagining themselves in an environment performing a specific activity using their senses (sight, hear, feel and smell). The images should have the athlete performing successfully and feeling satisfied with their performance.

☑ 3 Marks Questions

1. Explain the type of aggression in sports.
CBSE 2020

Ans. *There are two types of aggression in sports*

(*i*) **Instrumental Aggression** It is a type of aggression in which behaviour is directed at the target as a means to an end. For example, injuring a player to gain a competitive advantage or stopping an opponent from scoring.

(*ii*) **Hostile Aggression** It is a type of aggression in which behaviour is aimed toward another person who has angered or provoked the individual and is an end in itself. For example, hitting an opponent who has just been aggressive against the player. It is generally proceeded by anger.

2. What are the personality types as formulated by Carl Jung?

Ans. The personality type on mental basis is formulated by Carl Jung. *These are as follows*

(*i*) **Extroverts** Have more self-confidence, take more interest in others, are outgoing, lively and realistic.

They are very social and form friends quite easily. Actors, social and political leaders etc belong to this group.

(*ii*) **Introverts** Are too self-conscious, more interested in their own thoughts and ideas, self-centered, shy, reserved and lovers of solitude. They do not make friends easily and keep in the background on social occasions. Philosophers, poets, artists and scientists belong to this class.

(*iii*) **Ambiverts** Doubting whether people can be divided into these two extremes, he put most of the people in this category and they have been labelled as 'ambiverts.'

The ambiverts are a mixture of both the extremes in a balanced manner. Ambiverts are neither outgoing nor reserved to themselves. They are able to adjust themselves to any situation.

3. What is Self-esteem? State in brief.

Ans. In psychology, the term self-esteem is used to describe a person's overall subjective sense of personal worth. In other words, self-esteem may be defined as how much you appreciate and like yourself regardless of the circumstances. Your self-esteem is defined by many factors including self-confidence, feeling of security, identity, sense of belonging and feeling of competence.

Self-esteem impacts our decision-making process, relationships, emotional health, and our overall well-being. It also influences motivation, as sportspersons with a healthy, positive view of themselves understand their potential and may feel inspired to take on new challenges in sports.

4. Vijay is a football player of Kennedy school. He is famous for his aggressive play in the field. Because of his aggression he scored many goals. At the same time, he was punished for his aggressive behaviour with opponent.

(i) What level of aggression is needed in sports?
(a) Partially
(b) Fully
(c) No need
(d) None of the above

(ii) Hostile aggression is also known as .... aggression.
(a) Reactive
(b) Channelled
(c) Assertive
(d) Instrumental

(iii) Which of the following is the example of Trait Theory of personality?
(a) Sheldon's classification
(b) Jung Classification
(c) Personality   (d) Intrinsic

Ans. (i) - (a),   (ii) - (a),   (iii) - (b)

⤢ 5 Marks Questions

1. What are the personality traits according to the Big theory? **CBSE Term II 2022**

Ans. The 'big five' are the broad categories of five personality traits that are universal. *They are as follows*

(i) **Openness** It is a characteristic that includes imagination and insight. It leads to having a broad range of interests and being more adventurous when it comes to decision making. Creativity also plays a big part in the openness trait; this leads to a greater comfort zone when it comes to abstract and lateral thinking.

(ii) **Conscientiousness** It is a trait that includes high levels of thoughtfulness, good impulse control, and goal-directed behaviours.

This organised and structured approach is often found within people who work in science and even high-retail finance where detail orientation and organisation are required as a skill set. A highly conscientious person will regularly plan ahead and analyse their own behaviour to see how it affects others.

(iii) **Agreeableness** This trait includes signs of trust, altruism, kindness and affection. Highly agreeable people tend to have high prosocial behaviours which means that they are more inclined to be helping other people. Agreeable people tend to find careers in areas where they can help the most.

(iv) **Extraversion** It is characterised by excitability, sociability, talkativeness, assertiveness and high amounts of emotional expressiveness. People high in extraversion are extroverts and low in extraversion are introverts.

(v) **Neuroticism** Characteristics are sadness, moodiness and emotional instional instability. People high in this trait experience mood swings, anxiety, irritability and sadness. People low in this trait are more stable and emotionally resilient.

2. Explain the structure of personality. Describe the role of sports in developing the personality. **Delhi 2016**

Ans. The word personality is derived from Latin word *persona* meaning *the mask*. In ancient Greece, the actors used to wear masks to hide their identities while portraying their roles in a theatrical play. To an ordinary person the word personality conveys the meaning of one's physical appearance, his habits, his ways of dressing, his reputation, his manners and other similar characteristics.

So, personality basically reveals the psychological make-up of an individual through his behaviour.

In fact, it is the quality of a person's total behaviour. Physical activities and sports play an important role in the development of personality of an individual.

One of the primary and apparent aspects of one's personality is one's physical appearance. Children as well as adults, boys as well as girls, all are very much concerned about how they look. Physical activities are conducive to the growth and development of the physique. Robust and athletic physique does enhance one's personality. Poise, grace, agility and the manner one carries oneself have a great impact on one's personality.

CHAPTER 10

Training in Sports

Training is a process of preparing an individual for any event, activity or job. Usually in sports, we use the term sports training, which denotes the sense of preparing sportspersons for the highest level of performance.

According to **Mathew** (1981), "Sports training is the basic form of preparation of a sportsman."

Keeping in view the aim of sports training in competitive sports, the following objectives of sports training may be set to reach the aim

(*i*) Personality development
(*ii*) Physical fitness and development
(*iii*) Skill/ Technique development
(*iv*) Tactical development
(*v*) Mental Training

Talent Identification in Sports

Talent identification refers to the process of recognising current participants with the potential to become elite players. It entails predicting performance over time by measuring physical, physiological, psychological and sociological attributes as well as technical abilities, either in isolation or in combination.

As per other studies, talent identification in sport is a process in which individuals who are more likely to prosper in a given sport are identified according to the test of specific factors.

Utilisation of scientific methods to identify athletes with potential reduces time required to reach high performance, enhances the coach training effectiveness, increases competitiveness and number of athletes aiming to attain high level and increases confidence.

Talent Development in Sports

Talent development in sports is the most important stage in the process of achieving sporting success. It is aimed at providing the most optimal learning environment to help promising youth athletes realise their potential.

Optimum environment involves provision of adequate number of competent coaches, experts and managers, adequate and availability of quality facilities and equipment for training and testing as well as time for training, actual training and practice that are directed towards enhancing athletes' development.

Sports Training Cycles

There is a concept of periodisation in sports which includes three different training cycles.

Micro Cycles

A micro cycle is the shortest training cycle, typically lasting a week with the goal of facilitating a focused block of training. Each micro cycle is planned based on where it is in the overall macro cycle.

Micro cycles are to vary the levels of stress an athlete is subjected to throughout the week's training sessions. This would see a coach implementing sessions that focus on progressions, high volume or load as well as planned regeneration days.

- Monday - Low Intensity (70% load intensity)
- Tuesday - High Intensity (90-100%)
- Wednesday - Medium Intensity (80%)
- Thursday - Low Intensity (70%)
- Friday - Regeneration (60%)
- Saturday - Match Day
- Sunday - Regeneration/Rest Day (60%)

Meso Cycles

The meso cycle represents a specific block of training that is typically made up of 3-4 micro cycles (3-4weeks) that is designed to accomplish a particular goal. A meso cycle form a number of continuous weeks (micro cycles) where the training programme focuses towards improving the same physical adaptations, for example maximal strength, static strength, maximal speed or Functional Threshold Power (FTP).

Meso cycles are formed from 21-28 days. For an experienced athlete, a coach would focus on utilising the full 28 days and for an inexperienced athlete, a 21 day meso cycle.

Macro Cycles

A macro cycle is an annual plan that works towards peaking for the goal competition of the year. Macro cycles incorporate all 52 weeks of annoal plan.

There are three phases in the macro cycle

(*i*) **The Preparation Phase** It is further broken up into general and specific preparation. An example of general preparation would be building an aerobic base for an endurance athlete such as running on a treadmill or by working through multiple micro cycles on the track. An example of specific preparation would be to work on the proper form to be more efficient and to work more on the final format of the sport. This could be focusing on transition techniques with a triathlete.

(*ii*) **The Competitive Phase** It can be several competitions, which lead to the main competition. The competitive phase ends with tapering for the competition.

(*iii*) **The Transition Phase** It is important for psychological reasons, a year dedicating time towards training means some time off is just as important. An amateur athlete may take a couple of months off while a professional athlete might take as little as two weeks off.

Method to Develop

(A) Strength

Strength is the ability of a muscle to exert force in a single muscle contraction or it is the ability to overcome resistance. Strength is an essential component of physical fitness. *Types of strength are*

(*i*) Maximum strength

(*ii*) Explosive strength

(*iii*) Strength endurance

(*iv*) Static strength

Training Methods for Improving Strength

Training methods for improving strength are

(i) Isometric Exercises

An isometric contraction occurs when there is tension on a muscle but no movement is made, causing the length of the muscle to remain the same.

These isometric exercises were first introduced by Hettinger and Muller (1953). Examples of these exercises are pressing or pushing a wall, lifting a very heavy weight while holding a static position, pulling the rope in tug-of-war etc.

Advantages of isometric exercises are as follows

- Develop static strength.
- Need less time.
- Can be performed anywhere because no equipment is required.

Disadvantages of isometric exercises are as follows

- Muscles gain most strength at the angle used in exercise.
- Avoid if you have heart problems, as they cause a rise in blood pressure due to a drop in blood flow to the muscle during the contraction.

(ii) Isotonic Exercises

Isotonic exercise is a form of exercise which involves controlled contraction and extension of muscles and mobilisation of the joints around those muscles. Examples include a push-up or squat. These were developed by De Loone (1954).

Isotonic exercises are of two types

(*a*) Concentric   (*b*) Eccentric

Advantages of isotonic exercises are as follows

- Strengthens the muscle throughout the range of motion.
- Can be adapted easily to suit different sports.

Disadvantages of isotonic exercises are as follows

- Muscle soreness after exercise because of the high stress level.
- Muscles gain the dynamic strength when they are at their weakest point of action.

(iii) Isokinetic Exercises

Isokinetic exercises are performed on specially designed machines. These exercises were developed by Perrine in 1968.

In these exercises, there is movement along with continuous tension in both flexor and extensor muscles e.g. swimming, cycling etc.

Advantages of isokinetic exercises are as follows

- They develop a high level of dynamic as well as explosive strength.
- These are effective for almost every game.

Disadvantages of isokinetic exercises are as follows

- They require special types of equipment.
- They must be performed under observation of a coach.

(B) Endurance

Endurance is the ability to do sports movements with the desired quality and speed under conditions of fatigue. *Types of endurance are*

(*i*) **Aerobic Endurance** Aerobic means 'with oxygen.' During aerobic work, the body is working at a level that the demands for oxygen and fuel can be met by the body's intake.

(*ii*) **Anaerobic Endurance** During anaerobic (without oxygen) work involving maximum effort, the body is working so hard that the demands for oxygen and fuel exceed the rate of supply and the muscles have to rely on the stored reserves of fuel.

(*iii*) **Speed Endurance** Speed endurance is used to develop the coordination of muscle contraction.

(*iv*) **Strength Endurance** Strength endurance is used to develop the athlete's capacity to maintain the quality of his muscles' contractile force.

Advantages of endurance are as follows

- Needs only a small amount of easy to use, accessible equipment, if any.
- Good for aerobic fitness.
- Good for losing weight.

Disadvantages of endurance are as follows

- Can be boring.
- Does not improve anaerobic fitness, so it is not as good for team games like football or hockey which involve short bursts of speed.

Training Method for Endurance Development

Methods for endurance development are

(*i*) Continuous Training

(*ii*) Interval Training

(*iii*) Fartlek Training

Advantages of training method for endurance development are as follows

- It is good for increasing strength and cardiorespiratory endurance.
- Several athletics can take part in the training programme at a time.
- It does not require any equipment and can be organised easily.
- This training method is not rigid; it is flexible in nature.

Disadvantages of training method for endurance development are as follows

- The trainee does very hard training which is sometimes difficult to see his/her efforts making.

- Sometimes the athlete is likely to drop efforts.
- As it is not pre-planned so it may cause accidents.
- An appropriate check on trainees cannot be maintained.

(C) Speed

It is the ability to cover distance in minimum possible time or the ability to perform movement in the shortest possible time. It is the quickness of movement of body parts. Speed used in endurance is called speed endurance. It is the ability to do work faster. *Different types of speed are*

(*i*) Maximum speed

(*ii*) Explosive speed (power)

(*iii*) Speed endurance

Training Methods for Speed Development

A speed development programme can be framed according to need, level and training state of the players.

(*i*) **Acceleration Run** Acceleration runs are usually adopted to develop speed specially in attaining maximum speed from a stationary position.

(*ii*) **Pace Races or Run** Pace races mean running the whole distance of a race at a constant speed. In pace races, an athlete runs the race with uniform speed, generally 800 m and above.

Flexibility and Its Methods

Flexibility is the ability to perform a joint action through a range of movements. It is needed to perform everyday activities with relative ease.

Flexibility tends to deteriorate with age. Without adequate flexibility, daily activities are more difficult to perform. Being flexible significantly reduces the chance of experiencing occasional and chronic back pain.

There are two types of flexibility

(*i*) Passive flexibility

(*ii*) Active flexibility

Methods of flexibility development are as follows

(*i*) **Ballistic Method** It is the oldest form of doing stretching exercises. This method involves jerk in movement.

(*ii*) **Slow Stretching Method** In this method the muscle or joint involved is stretched to the maximum possible limit using slow movement.

(*iii*) **Slow Stretching and Holding Method** It is the extension of slow stretching method.

(*iv*) **Post-Isometric Stretching** This method of flexibility development is based on the principle of proprioceptive neuromuscular facilitation.

Coordinative Abilities

Coordination is one of the main components of physical fitness. It is the ability to perform smooth and accurate movements involving different parts of the body. It requires good awareness of relative limb and body positions, and good integration between the senses and muscles involved in the movement.

Different types of coordinative abilities are

(*i*) Differentiation ability

(*ii*) Orientation ability   (*iii*) Coupling ability

(*iv*) Reaction ability   (*v*) Balance ability

(*vi*) Rhythm ability   (*vii*) Adaptation ability

Previous Years'

Examination & Other Important Questions

☑ 1 Mark Questions (MCQ)

1. While exercising on a multigym, the type of muscular contraction that occurs is
CBSE 2020
(a) Isotonic   (b) Isometric
(c) Isokinetic   (d) Eccentric

Ans. *(b)* Isometric

2. Which of the following is not a type of strength?
(a) Minimum strength
(b) Maximum strength
(c) Explosive strength
(d) Strength endurance

Ans. *(a)* Minimum strength

3. A micro cycle is the shortest training cycle, typically lasting
(a) a day   (b) a week
(c) a month   (d) a year

Ans. *(b)* a week

4. A push up is which form of exercise?
(a) Isokinetic   (b) Isotonic
(c) Isometric   (d) Aerobic

Ans. *(b)* Isotonic

5. Which of the following is not an objective of sports training?
(a) Technique development
(b) Tactical development
(c) Physical fitness
(d) Aerobic endurance training

Ans. *(d)* Aerobic endurance training

6. A disadvantage of isometric exercises is that ....
(a) muscles become sore after the exercise
(b) they require special equipment
(c) they cannot be done by heart patients
(d) None of the above

Ans. *(c)* they cannot be done by heart patients

7. Which are two forms of isotonic exercises?
(a) Concentric and eccentric
(b) Static and dynamic
(c) Speed and strength
(d) Continuous and with intervals

Ans. *(a)* Concentric and eccentric

8. Which of the following is an advantage of doing isokinetic exercises?
(a) They strengthen the muscles throughout their range of motion.
(b) They can be performed anywhere because no special equipment is required.
(c) They are simple to perform and so do not require coaching.
(d) They develop both dynamic and explosive strength.

Ans. *(d)* They develop both dynamic and explosive strength.

9. During anaerobic endurance, the body's demand for oxygen and fuel is .... the rate of their supply.
(a) more than   (b) less than
(c) equal to   (d) Both (b) and (c)

Ans. *(a)* more than

10. Training for endurance development has the advantage of ....
(a) flexibility
(b) being good for increasing strength
(c) not requiring any special equipment
(d) All of the above

Ans. *(d)* All of the above

11. Which of the following is not a training method for endurance development?
(a) Fartlek Training
(b) Continuous Training
(c) Interval Training
(d) None of the above

Ans. *(d)* None of the above

12. Different types of speed which need to be developed in an athlete include ....
(a) maximum, minimum and average
(b) maximum, explosive and speed endurance
(c) maximum, ballistic and explosive
(d) None of the above

Ans. *(b)* maximum, explosive and speed endurance

13. Out of the following methods, which one is not used for development of flexibility?
(a) Slow stretching
(b) Post-Isometric stretching
(c) Back flexibility exercises
(d) Ballistic

Ans. *(c)* Back flexibility exercises

14. Which of the following is not a coordinative ability?
(a) Rhythm   (b) Balance
(c) Coupling   (d) None of these

Ans. *(d)* None of the above

☑ 1 Mark Questions (VSA)

1. Which method will you suggest to develop endurance? **CBSE 2019**

Ans. To develop endurance, we can use any one of the training methods called Continuous Training, Interval Training or Fartlek Training.

2. Explain the term sports training.
CBSE 2018

Ans. Sports training is the physical, intellectual, technical, psychological and moral preparation of an athlete or a player by means of physical exercises.

3. What does the term 'Fartlek' mean and who developed this training method?
All India 2017

Ans. Fartlek is a Swedish term which means 'speed play' and has been used by distance runner for years. Fartlek is a form of road running or cross country running in which the runner usually changes the pace significantly during the run.

This method was introduced by O Astrand and Gosta Halner. It is good for aerobic and anaerobic fitness. That is why it makes an athlete a better sprinter and a better long-distance runner.

4. What are pace races? **CBSE 2013**

Ans. Pace races mean running the whole distance of a race at a constant speed. In pace races, an athlete runs the race with uniform speed, generally 800m and above.

Very young children can maintain their maximum speed for 15 to 20m, whereas a well-trained athlete can maintain maximum speed for 40m. Repetitions can be fixed according to the standard of the athletes.

5. What do you mean by training?

Ans. Training means to prepare someone for some assignment. Training is the process of preparation for some task.

6. Write any two definitions of sports training.

Ans. According to **Mathew,** "Sports training is the basic form of preparation of a sportsman."

According to **Martin,** "It is a planned and controlled process to achieve goals in which the changes of motor performance and behaviour are made through measures of content, methods and organisation."

7. What are the methods for developing flexibility?

Ans. *Methods for developing flexibility are*
- Ballistic method
- Slow-stretching method
- Slow-stretching and Holding method
- Post-Isometric stretching method

☑ 3 Marks Questions

1. Differentiate isometric and isotonic exercises. **CBSE 2021, CBSE 2020, Delhi 2016**

Ans. An isometric contraction occurs when there is tension on a muscle without any movement. The length of the muscles remains constant.

Isotonic exercises involve controlled contraction and extension of muscles and mobilisation of the joints around those muscles.

A comparison between their characteristics is given below

Isometric Exercises	Isotonic Exercises
Less or no equipment required.	Sometimes equipment is required to perform them.
It develops static strength.	It develops dynamic strength.
It needs less time.	Muscles which are used in this exercise gain most strength.

2. Explain interval training method.
All India 2017

or Discuss any two methods of endurance development.

Ans. (*i*) **Interval Training Method** It is a type of training that involves a series of low to high intensity exercise workouts interspersed with rest of relief periods. The high intensity periods are typically at or close to anaerobic exercise, while the recovery periods involve activity of lower intensity.

(*ii*) **Fartlek Training Method** Fartlek is a training method that blends continuous training with interval training. It is a form of speed training that can be effective in improving individual's speed and endurance. Many runners, especially beginners enjoy fartlek training because it involves speed work. It is more flexible and not as demanding as traditional interval training. Another benefit is that it can be done on all types of terrains–roads, trails or even hills.

3. What is strength? Discuss any two types of exercises used for strength development **All India 2016**

or Explain what is strength and write the methods of improving strength.

Ans. Strength is the ability of a muscle to exert force in single muscle contraction or it is the ability to overcome resistance. Strength is an essential component of physical fitness.

Types of exercises for strength development are

(*i*) **Isometric Exercises** 'Iso' means 'constant' and 'metric' means 'length'. An isometric contraction occurs when there is tension on a muscle but no movement is made, causing the length of the muscle to remain the same.

(*ii*) **Isotonic Exercise** Isotonic exercise is a form of exercise which involves controlled contraction and extension of muscles and mobilisation of the joints around those muscles.

(*iii*) **Isokinetic Exercises** Isokinetic exercises are performed on specially designed machines. These exercises were developed by Perrine in 1968. In these exercises, there is movement along with continuous tension in both flexor and extensor muscles.

4. Define speed. Explain the methods of speed development. **Delhi 2016, 2015**

or How do acceleration runs and pace races develop speed?

Ans. Speed is the ability of an individual to cover maximum distance in minimum possible time.

Developing Methods

(*i*) **Acceleration Run** Acceleration runs are usually adopted to develop speed specially in attaining maximum speed from a stationary position. Before acceleration runs, proper warm up must be done. After every acceleration run, there should be a proper interval so that the athlete may start the next run without any fatigue. Generally, the athlete should take rest of 4 to 5 minutes in between the runs.

(*ii*) **Pace Races** Pace races mean running the whole distance of a race at a constant speed. In pace races, an athlete runs the race with uniform speed, generally 800 m and above. Very young children can maintain their maximum speed for 15 to 20m, whereas a well-trained athlete can maintain maximum speed for 40m. Repetitions can be fixed according to the standard of the athletes.

5. Briefly explain different types of coordinative abilities. **All India 2016**

Ans. *The different types of coordinative abilities are*

(*i*) **Differentiation Ability** It is the ability to achieve a high level of fine tuning or harmony of individual movement phases and body part movements.

(*ii*) **Orientation Ability** It is the ability to determine and change the position and movements of the body in time and space in relation to a definite of action e.g. playing field, boxing ring, apparatus and a moving object e.g. ball, opponent, partner.

(*iii*) **Coupling Ability** It is the ability to coordinate body part movements (e.g. movements of hand, feet, trunk etc) with one another and in relation to a definite goal-oriented whole body movement. Coupling ability is especially important in sports in which movements with a high degree of difficulty have to be done e.g. gymnastics, team games.

(*iv*) **Reaction Ability** It is the ability to react quickly and effectively to a signal.

(*v*) **Balance Ability** It is the ability to maintain balance during whole body movements and to regain balance quickly after balance disturbing movements.

(*vi*) **Rhythm Ability** It is the ability to perceive an externally given rhythm and to reproduce it in motor action.

(*vii*) **Adaptation Ability** It is the ability to adjust or completely change the movement programme during movement on the basis of changes or anticipated changes in the situation.

6. Explain the physiological factors determining speed. **Delhi 2016**

or What are various factors of speed?

or Explain the types of speed.

or Write in brief about any three physiological factors determining speed.

Ans. *The various factors of speed are*

(*i*) **Reaction Speed** It is the ability to respond to a given stimulus as quickly as possible. In sports, reaction ability is not only significant to react quickly to a signal, but it should also be accurate according to situation.

(*ii*) **Movement Speed** It is the ability to do a single movement in the minimum time. Movement speed is of high relevance in sports like jumping, throwing, kicking, boxing etc.

(*iii*) **Acceleration Speed** It is the ability to increase speed from minimum to maximum. This form of speed, to a great extent, depends upon explosive strength, frequency of movement and technique. This ability is important in swimming, hockey, football, gymnastics etc.

(*iv*) **Locomotor Ability** It can be defined as the ability to maintain maximum speed of locomotion over a period of time as far as possible. This ability is very important in races, speed skating, swimming, hockey, football etc.

(*v*) **Speed Endurance** It is the ability to do sports movements with high speed under conditions of fatigue. Speed endurance is a combination of speed and endurance abilities. This ability depends upon anaerobic capacity, psychic factors and level of skill.

7. Suggest different ways to improve reaction ability of a player. **CBSE 2013**

Ans. Improved reaction ability is a performance prerequisite to do motor actions under given conditions in minimum time. There are two methods for improving this.

They are

(*i*) **Acceleration Runs** They test the ability to achieve high speed of locomotion from a stationary position or from a slow moving position.

Acceleration ability is improved indirectly by improving on explosive strength, technique and movement frequency.

(*ii*) **Pace Races** Pace races mean running the whole distance of a race at a constant speed. In pace races, an athlete runs the race with uniform speed, generally 800 m and above. Very young children can maintain their maximum speed for 15 to 20m, whereas a well-trained athletes can maintain maximum speed for 40m. Repetitions can be fixed according to the standard of the athletes.

8. Explain the advantages of Fartlek training. **CBSE 2012**

Ans. *Advantages of Fartlek training are*

* It is good for increasing strength and cardiorespiratory endurance.
* Several athletics can take part in the training programme at a time.
* It does not require any equipment and can be organised easily.
* This training method is not rigid; it is flexible in nature.
* It improves the efficiency of the heart and lungs.
* It provides experience of nature.

9. What do you mean by talent identification in sports?

Ans. Talent identification refers to the process of recognising current participants with the potential to become elite players. It entails predicting performance over time by measuring physical, physiological, psychological and sociological attributes as well as technical abilities, either in isolation or in combination.

10. Prasad is coaching a football team for which he had designed a training programme. During the training programme he noticed that some of the players were very good shooters, but they were lacking stamina or endurance. Thus, they were getting tired very easily. So Prasad tried to enhance the endurance level of these players by using different methods during the training programme.

Based on the above passage, answer the questions given below.

(*i*) The players were lacking with which component of physical fitness in them?

(*ii*) To develop the capability to resist fatigue in the players, which type of training will you suggest?

(*iii*) What values are shown by Prasad?

Ans. (*i*) They were lacking in stamina or endurance.

(*ii*) To develop the capability to resist fatigue in the players, I will suggest for both continuous training and interval training.

(*iii*) The values shown by Prasad are dedication to his duty and motivation for improving his team's performance.

11. Sunita, a student of class VIII, was identified as a strong girl both physically and mentally. She is being encouraged by her teacher to take up wrestling as a professional sport and start training. Sunita is also interested in the sport as she has been watching the sport on the T.V and she is highly impressed by the Indian women wrestlers. She expresses her interest to her family that she wants to learn boxing but her brothers made fun of her and ridiculed her. Her father on seeing her interest sent her to a professional coach to learn that sport properly.

(i) Which component of physical fitness is most important for a sport like wrestling?
(a) Speed   (b) Strength
(c) Endurance   (d) Flexibility

(ii) Which type of body type is most suited for wrestling?
(a) Ectomorph   (b) Mesomorph
(c) Micromorph   (d) Endomorph

(iii) Which type of training method is used to develop strength?
(a) Interval Training
(b) Iso metric Training
(c) Ballistic Method
(d) Acceleration Runs

Ans. (i) - (b),   (ii) - (b),   (iii) - (b)

12. Ravi has the aim of joining any of the uniform services like police, army, air force etc. But he has not qualified the 1500m run in their selection criteria. Without qualifying this run, he can't go for the next level.

(i) 1500m run is conducted to find the
(a) Endurance ability (b) Speed
(c) Strength   (d) Explosive

(ii) The best training method for development of endurance is
(a) Continuous training method
(b) Interval training method
(c) Circuit training method
(d) Fartlek training method

(iii) In Interval training method is based on principle of ....
(a) Over load   (b) Effort
(c) Effort and Recovery (d) Recovery

Ans. (i) - (a),   (ii) - (a),   (iii) - (c)

13. Raghu was good thrower. When he joined a new training camp, where he observed some athletes were running on uneven surfaces like bushes, rocks, pits etc. He was in dilemma. Then the coach explained about that training in detail.

(i) What type of training are they doing?
(a) Fartlek training
(b) Ballistic method
(c) Interval training
(d) Acceleration run

(ii) Stretching exercise improves ....
(a) Flexibility   (b) Strength
(c) Coordination   (d) Explosive

(iii) Fartlek training is also known as
(a) Pace runs   (b) Speed play
(c) Acceleration run   (d) 400 m run

Ans. (i) - (a),   (ii) - (a),   (iii) - (b)

☑ 5 Marks Questions

1. Discuss about three phases of macro cycle.
CBSE 2019

Ans. A macro cycle is an annual plan that works towards peaking for the goal competition of the year. There are three phases in the macro cycle such as:

(i) **The preparation phase** It is further broken up into general and specific preparation. An example of general preparation would be building an aerobic base for an endurance athlete such as running on a treadmill or by working through multiple micro cycles on the track.

An example of specific preparation would be to work on the proper form to be more efficient and to work more on the final format of the sport. This could be focusing on transition techniques with a triathlete.

(ii) **The competitive phase** It can be several competitions, which lead to the main competition. The competitive phase ends with tapering for the competition.

(iii) **The transition phase** It is important for psychological reasons, a year dedicating time towards training means some time off is just as important. An amateur athlete may take a couple of months off while a professional athlete might take as little as two weeks off.

2. What do you understand by Coordinative ability? Discuss about different types of coordinative abilities. **CBSE 2019**

Ans. The ability to control the movements of different parts of our body so that they work well together is called coordinative ability.

For different types of coordinative abilities, refer to Q. No. 5 (3 Marks Questions) on page no. 102 and 103.

3. Write in detail about strength improving methods–Isometric, Isotonic and Isokinetic. **CBSE 2019**

or Define strength. Explain the details of strength training methods with the advantages and disadvantages of each. **CBSE 2012**

Ans. Strength is the ability of our muscles to overcome resistance.

We use the following methods of strength development

(i) **Isometric Exercises** 'Iso' means 'constant' and 'metric' means 'length'. An isometric contraction occurs when there is tension on a muscle but no movement is made, causing the length of the muscle to remain the same.

Advantages of Isometric
- Develops static strength.
- Needs less time.
- Can be performed anywhere because no equipment is required.

Disadvantages of Isometric
- Muscles gain most strength at the angle used in exercise.

- Avoid if you have heart problems as they cause a rise in blood pressure due to a drop in blood flow to the muscle during the contraction.

(ii) **Isotonic Exercises** Isotonic exercise is a form of exercise which involves controlled contraction and extension of muscles and mobilisation of the joints around those muscles.

Advantages of Isotonic
- Strengthens the muscle throughout the range of motion.
- Can be adapted easily to suit different sports.

Disadvantages of Isotonic
- Muscle soreness after exercise because of the high stress level.
- Muscles gain the dynamic strength when they are at their weakest point of action.

(iii) **Isokinetic Exercises** Isokinetic exercises are performed on specially designed machines. These exercises were developed by Perrine in 1968. In these exercises, there is movement along with continuous tension in both flexor and extensor muscles.

Advantages of Isokinetic
- They develop a high level of dynamic as well as explosive strength.
- These are effective for almost every game.

Disadvantages of Isokinetic
- They require special types of equipment.
- They must be performed under observation of a coach.

4. Define flexibility and explain the methods of flexibility development. **Delhi 2015**

Ans. Flexibility is the range of movement. It is the ability of joints to move in the maximum range.

Developing methods of flexibility are

(i) **Ballistic Method** It is the oldest form of doing stretching exercises. This method involves jerk in movement. A joint or muscle is stretched with just rhythmic actions or movements around a joint. Before performing such exercise, the appropriate warm-up is essential.

(ii) **Slow-Stretching Method** In this method, the muscle or joint involved is stretched to the maximum possible limit using slow movement. It has an advantage over the ballistic method as it minimises the chances of overstretching of the muscle or joint, preventing injury to the tissue.

(*iii*) **Slow-Stretching and Holding Method** It is the extension of slow- stretching method. Here the muscle is stretched to its maximum limit and then the position is held for few seconds before returning to the original position.

(*iv*) **Post-Isometric Stretching** This method of flexibility development is based on the principle of proprioceptive neuromuscular facilitation. In this procedure, the muscle is first contracted maximally for 6-8 seconds using isometric method. Then the muscle is gradually stretched to its maximum limit and is held in this position for 8-10 seconds. This process is to be repeated 4 to 8 times for each muscle group.

5.

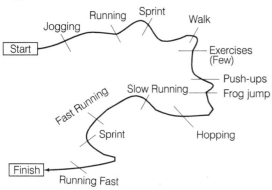

(i) From the above picture, it is identified as .... training method. **CBSE QB 2021**
(a) Pace runs   (b) Fartlek
(c) Isometric   (d) Isotonic

(ii) The above training method helps in increasing the ....
(a) Strength   (b) Speed
(c) Endurance   (d) Flexibility

(iii) The Swedish word meaning 'Speed Play' is ....
(a) Citius   (b) Fartlek
(c) Pace   (d) Altius

(iv) In the above training method, plays an important role
(a) Self-discipline   (b) Coach
(c) Guidance   (d) Support

(v) This training method was developed by
(a) Holmer   (b) Fartlek
(c) Robert   (d) Johnson
Ans. (i) - (b), (ii) - (c), (iii) - (b), (iv) - (a), (v) - (a)

6. Mr. Gopichand is a renowned badminton coach. When he started his academy, he selected our school badminton players and designed a training program. During the training, he noted that few players were good in defense but due to lack of endurance and strength, they were unable to play up to the last moment. He used various methods to enhance their endurance and strength. **CBSE QB 2021**

(i) This type of training and exercises help in increasing the static strength and maximal strength.
(a) Isometric
(b) Isotonic
(c) Isokinetic
(d) Aerobic

(ii) Isotonic exercise helps in enhancing
(a) Speed
(b) Strength
(c) Agility
(d) Endurance

(iii) High pressure over muscles can be seen in these set of exercises
(a) Isometric
(b) Isotonic
(c) Both (a) and (b)
(d) Ballistic

(iv) This training method is considered as best method to develop endurance
(a) Interval   (b) Continuous
(c) Fartlek   (d) Pace runs

(v) This endurance training method involves periods of hard work followed by a time period of rest repeatedly.
(b) Interval
(b) Continuous
(c) Fartlek
(d) Pace runs
Ans. (i) - (a), (ii) - (b), (iii) - (c), (iv) - (a), (v) - (a)

SAMPLE QUESTION PAPERS (1-3)

Sample Paper 1

Physical Education (Solved)

(A Highly Simulated Practice Question Paper for CBSE Class XII Examination)

General Instructions
- The question paper consists of 30 questions.
- All questions are compulsory.
- Question 1-12 (Multiple Choice Questions) carry 1 mark each.
- Question 13-16 carrying 2 marks each should be in approximately 30-50 words.
- Question 17-26 carrying 3 marks each should be in approximately 75-100 words.
- Question 27-30 carrying 5 marks each should be in approximately 155-200 words.

Time : 3 hours   **Max. Marks : 80**

1. Scoliosis may occur due to .... (1)
   - (a) paralysis of spinal muscles on one side
   - (b) one leg being short in length
   - (c) Carrying heavy loads on one shoulder
   - (d) Any of the above

or Which of the following is not a cause of flat foot deformity?
   - (a) Body heaviness
   - (b) Standing for a long time
   - (c) Lack of vitamin D and calcium
   - (d) Faulty posture

2. Which mineral is required for developing strong bones and teeth? (1)
   - (a) Copper
   - (b) Potassium
   - (c) Sodium
   - (d) Phosphorus

3. Which of the following Laws of Motion given by Sir Issac Newton is also known as 'Law of Inertia'? (1)
   - (a) Second Law
   - (b) Third Law
   - (c) First Law
   - (d) None of these

or The major asanas which should be practised to control obesity are Tadasana, Pawanmuktasana, ... and Ardh Matsyendrasana.

(a) Bhujangasana   (b) Trikonasana
(c) Halasana   (d) Paschimottanasana

4. In which type of menstrual dysfunction, tight or infrequent menstruation is witnessed by the woman?   (1)

(a) Premenstrual syndrome   (b) Amenorrhea
(c) Oligomenorrhea   (d) Premenstrual dysphoric disorder

5. Which country hosted summer Deaflympics in 1939?   (1)

(a) United States   (b) Italy
(c) Sweden   (d) Austria

6. 'Speed play' is another name of which method?   (1)

(a) Interval Method   (b) Continuous Method
(c) Isokinetic Method   (d) Fartlek Method

7. Which of the following is not the type of speed?   (1)

(a) Maximum speed   (b) Minimum speed
(c) Explosive speed   (d) Speed endurance

or A push up is which form of exercise?

(a) Isokinetic   (b) Isotonic
(c) Isometric   (d) Aerobic

8. .... method is used for drawing up fixtures in league type tournament.   (1)

(a) Cyclic   (b) Double league
(c) Round robin   (d) Single league

9. Which one of the following is not a component of physical fitness?   (1)

(a) Agility   (b) Anaerobic capacity
(c) Flexibility   (d) Muscle composition

10. Resistance against fatigue is called   (1)

(a) Strength   (b) Speed
(c) Endurance   (d) Agility

11. Assertion-Reason   (1)

Assertion (A) Biomechanics aims to achieve performance enhancement in sports.
Reason (R) Qualitative analysis helps in technique improvement and injury prevention.

In context of above two statements, which one of the following is correct?

Codes

(a) Both A and R are true and R is the correct explanation of A
(b) Both A and R are true, but R is not the correct explanation of A
(c) A is true, but R is false
(d) A is false, but R is true

12. Match List I with List II   (1)

	List I		List II
A.	Knock Knee	1.	Lack of exercise
B.	Lordosis	2.	Lack of Vitamin D
C.	Flat Foot	3.	Heredity defects
D.	Scoliosis	4.	Faulty Posture

Codes
(a) A-2, B-1, C-3, D-4   (b) A-2, B-1, C-4, D-3
(c) A-4, B-3, C-2, D-1   (d) A-4, B-1, C-3, D-2

13. Identify the below given asana and write the name.   (2)

(a)    (b)

(c)    (d)

14. Identify the below given deformities and write their names.   (2)

(a)    (b)

(c) 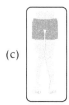   (d)

15. Suggest exercises, a corrective measures for curing Lordosis.   (2)

16. Differentiate between Extroverts and Introverts.   (2)

or Differentiate between Instrumental aggression and Hostile aggression.

17. Below given is the BMI data of a Boys Hostel's health check up.   (3)

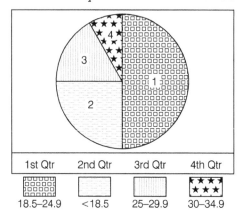

On the basis of the above data; answer the following questions:

(i) In which category does the minimum boys population falls into?

(a) Obese   (b) Normal weight
(c) Under weight   (d) Over weight

(ii) The hostel has to develop an activity based program to decrease the number of

(a) [ ]   (b) [★★★★/★★★]   (c) [▦]   (d) [▨]

(iii) Which category is related to under weight?

(a) [★★]   (b) [▨]   (c) [▦]   (d) [ ]

18. Below given is the Tournament fixture procedure of a CBSE Football National competition.

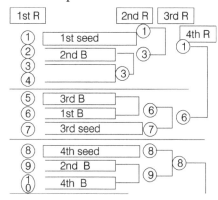

On the basis of the above data, answer the following questions.

(i) What is the number of Non-Seeded Teams in the Tournament?

(a) 04   (b) 09
(c) 12   (d) 07

(ii) The provision which places good teams in separate halves or pools so that they do not play with other good teams at earlier Rounds is known as ....
    (a) Bye   (b) League tournament
    (c) Seeding method   (d) Knock out tournament
(iii) Which of the following is not a Seeded Team?
    (a) Team 10   (b) Team 08
    (c) Team 13   (d) Team 07

19. Compare the injuries caused by abrasion and incision.   **(3)**

or Explain briefly strain and sprain.

20. Write the procedure of Flamingo Balance Test.   **(3)**

21. Write a short note on how Paralympics started.   **(3)**

or Explain in detail about Special Olympics.

22. List any three pre-meet responsibilities taken by sports committees.   **(3)**

23. What do you mean by balanced diet and nutrition? Explain.   **(3)**

24. Explain any three personality types of Big Five theory.   **(3)**

25. Briefly explain different types of coordinative abilities.   **(3)**

26. Briefly explain the functions and resources of fat soluble vitamins.   **(3)**

or Explain any three essential elements of diet.

27. (i) List any three benefits of performing Yogic *asanas*.

(ii) Explain the procedure for performing *Paschimottasana*.   **(5)**

28. Discuss the physiological factors determining components of Physical fitness.   **(5)**

or What are the effects of exercising on the cardiorespiratory system? Explain.

29. Explain the procedure of Chair Sit and Reach Test for senior citizens.   **(5)**

or What is the procedure of measuring height in Body Mass Index?

30. Pinki is appointed as a sports coach. She begins her training by measuring the cardiovascular fitness of all the athletes. Which test she administers and why? Explain its procedure.   **(5)**

ANSWERS

1. (*d*) Any of the above

   or (*c*) Lack of vitamin D and calcium

2. (*d*) Phosphorus

3. (*c*) First Law   *or*   (*d*) Paschimottanasana

4. (*c*) Oligomenorrhea

5. (*c*) Sweden

6. (*d*) Fartlek Method

7. (*b*) Minimum speed   *or*   (*b*) Isotonic

8. (*a*) Cyclic

9. (*b*) Anaerobic capacity

10. (*c*) Endurance

11. (*a*) Both A and R are true and R is the correct explanation of A

12. (*b*) 2143

13. (*a*) Ardha Matsyendrasana   (*b*) Bhujangasana

    (*c*) Paschimottanasana   (*d*) Pavanamuktasana

14. (a) Flat foot   (b) Scoliosis

    (c) Knock-Knees   (d) Lordosis

15. The exercises are as follows:

    - Lying in prone position, raise lower back region by keeping hands under abdomen, hips and shoulders down.

    - Lying in prone position, push torso (upper portion of body) up by keeping pelvic region on the floor and palms flat on the floor.

    - Sitting on a chair, bend and reach to the floor with shoulders positioning between the knees.

16.

	Extroverts	Introverts
(i)	They are very social outgoing, confident, lively and make friends easily.	They are reserved, too self-conscious and more interested in their own thoughts and ideas.
(ii)	Actors politicians group leaders are extroverts	Poets, artists, writers, philosophers are introverts usually.

or

	Instrumental Aggression	Hostile Aggression
(i)	It is a positive kind of aggression as aim is to achieve a goal/target.	It is a negative kind of aggression as aim is to cause harm or injury to others.
(ii)	It arises from the need to excel and to do better.	It arises from insult, hurt bad feelings, jealousy and threat.

17. (*i*) (i) (b) Normal weight

(ii) (b) ★★★

(iii) (d) ▭

18. (i) (b) 09   (ii) (c) Seeding method

(iii) (a) Team 10

19. ● Abrasion and incision are types of soft tissue injuries. Abrasion is a wound caused when the skin is scraped or rubbed in the epidermis (upper layer of the skin). This injury is commonly caused by sliding, slip over surface etc. Whereas, incision is a cut or a wound produced by cutting with a scalpel (sharp knife). Incision is a surgical procedure which the doctors may perform.

● Abrasion causes severe pain and sometimes bleeding over affected part whereas, blood usually comes out freely from incision.

● Abrasion can be often caused by both sharp blunt object and is deep. Abrasion can even be treated at home but incision injury of serious nature needs immediate medical attention otherwise can be fatal.

or

Strain and sprain are two common soft tissue injuries. Strain is caused due to twist, pull or tear of the muscles or tendons with symptoms of pain, swelling and loss of muscle strength.

On the other hand, sprain is a partial or complete tear of a ligament with symptoms of pain, swelling, bruising, loss of function. Both are caused due to weak muscular systems or insufficient warming up.

20. *Procedures of Flamingo Balance Test are*

● Stand on the beam. Keep balance by holding the instructor's hand (if required to start).

● While balancing on the preferred leg, the free leg is flexed at the knee and the foot of this leg held close to the buttocks.

● Start the watch as the instructor lets go of the participant/subject.

● Pause the stopwatch each time the subject loses balance (either by falling off the beam or letting goes of the foot being held).

● Resume over, again timing until they lose balance. Count the number of falls in 60 seconds of balancing.

● If there are more than 15 falls in the first 30 seconds, the test is terminated.

21. Paralympics were started due to the efforts of Dr Ludwig Tuttmann. He was a neurologist who treated British war casualties during World War II. He founded the National Spinal Injuries Centre at Stoke Mandeville Hospital in England.

Then in July 1948, Guttmann organised a sports competition for patients with spinal cord injuries which became immensely popular. This was the first event of this type after which the Paralympics were organised regularly every four years.

or

Special Olympics is the World's largest organisation for children and adults with intellectual disabilities and physical disabilities.

The pioneer of special Olympics was Eunice Mary Kennedy Shriver. The idea of Special Olympics was born out of Shriver' experience of witnessing the social exclusion of people with intellectual disabilities who were placed in custodial institutions.

Due to her sincere effort, the first Special Olympic games were held in Chicago in July, 1968. The US Olympic Committee in 1971, gave the Special Olympics an official approval to use the name 'Olympics'.

The United Nations declared 1986 as the year of 'Special Olympics'. The logo of Special Olympics is based on the sculpture 'Joy and Happiness to all Children of the World'.

22. Three pre-meet responsibilities taken by sports committees are as follows :

   (i) Meeting to important officials to fix the venue, date and timings of the sports event.

   (ii) To prepare a list of events, ceremonies and entertainment programmes that will be covered during the event.

   (iii) To appoint different officials that are going to judge the sports events as well as invite a chief guest.

23. **Balance Diet** A balanced diet is that which contains the proper amount of each nutrient. A balanced diet consists of all essential food constituents i.e. protein, carbohydrates, fats, vitamins and minerals in correct proportion. Salient features of balanced diet are as follows

   • A balance diet must contain all the essential constituents in adequate amount.

   • There must be definite proportion between the different constituents of food.

   • The food should be easily digestible.

   Nutrition It is a dynamic process in which the body is made healthy by the consumption of food. It is the essential substances or the chemical compositions present int he food that are essential for the growth and replacement of tissues. If a person takes proper nutrition, he/she will be physically fit and healthy.

24. Three personality types of Big five theory are

   (i) **Openness** It is a characteristic that includes imagination and insight. It leads to having a broad range of interests and being more adventurous when it comes to decision making. Creativity also plays a big part in the openness trait; this leads to a greater comfort zone when it comes to abstract and lateral thinking.

   (ii) **Conscientiousness** It is a trait that includes high levels of thoughtfulness, good impulse control, and goal-directed behaviours.

   This organised and structured approach is often found within people who work in science and even high-retail finance where detail orientation and organisation are required as a skill set. A highly conscientious person will regularly plan ahead and analyse their own behaviour to see how it affects others.

(iii) **Agreeableness** This trait includes signs of trust, altruism, kindness and affection. Highly agreeable people tend to have high prosocial behaviours which means that they are more inclined to be helping other people. Agreeable people tend to find careers in areas where they can help the most.

25. The different types of coordinative abilities are :

   (i) **Differentiation Ability** It is the ability to achieve a high level of fine tuning or harmony of individual movement phases and body part movements.

   (ii) **Orientation Ability** It is the ability to determine and change the position and movements of the body in different types of situations. For example, in gymnastics, the position and movement of head and eyes is important for orientation.

   (iii) **Coupling Ability** It is the ability to coordinate body part movements (e.g. movements of hand, feet, trunk etc) with one another.

   Coupling ability is especially important in sports in which movements with a high degree of difficulty have to be done e.g. gymnastics, team games etc.

26. The vitamins that are soluble in fats are called fat soluble vitamins. They are vitamin A, D, E and K.

   Functions

   - **Vitamin A** This is essential for normal growth of the body. Deficiency of vitamin A leads to night blindness and also affects the kidneys, nervous system and digestive system.
     Sources are milk, curd, ghee, egg yolk, fish, tomato, papaya, green vegetables, orange, spinach, carrot and pumpkin.

   - **Vitamin D** This is essential for the formation of healthy teeth and bones. The presence of this vitamin in the body enables it to absorb calcium and phosphorus. Its deficiency causes rickets, softness of bones, teeth diseases.
     Sources are egg yolk, fish, sunlight, vegetables, cod liver oil, milk, cream, butter.

   - **Vitamin E** This is essential in increasing the fertility among men and women as well as proper functioning of adrenal and sex glands. Its deficiency causes weakness in muscles and heart.
     Sources are green vegetables, sprouts, coconut oil, dry and fresh fruits, milk, meat, butter, maize.

   or

   There are many nutrients in the food. These are known as elements. *Essential elements of our diet are*

   (*i*) **Carbohydrates** These are the compounds of carbon, hydrogen and oxygen.
   Sources Fruits, milk, vegetables, pulses, bajra, rice, cakes, etc.
   Functions The main function of carbohydrates is to provide energy to the body, brain and nervous system.

(*ii*) **Proteins** Proteins are a chain of amino acids that contain carbon, oxygen, hydrogen and nitrogen.

Sources Eggs, milk, meat, beans, animal products, etc.

Functions Proteins are the main components of muscles, organs and glands. The cells of muscles and ligaments are maintained with protein and proteins are used for the growth and development of children.

(*iii*) **Fats** Fats contain carbon, hydrogen and oxygen.

Sources Animal products, milk, cream, cheese, butter, olive oil, etc.

Functions Fats are a source of energy. They are important for the proper functioning of the body. Fatty acids provide the raw materials which help in control of blood pressure.

27. (i) Three benefits of performing Yogic asanas are : stimulating blood circulation, balancing the nervous system and relieving stress.

(ii) The procedure for performing Paschimottasana are :

(a) Lie down on your back on a mat with your legs straight and stretch your hands upward straight besides the ears. Your fingers should be straight.

(b) Inhale deeply and slowly raise up the trunk and sit. You should keep your hands beside the ears.

(c) In this step, exhale and bend the body from the hips while keeping the shoulders open and the head up. Reach forward and hold the first fingers in your legs with the index fingers and the middle fingers of your hands.

(d) Deeply inhale and exhale once. Now, our elbows should be beside the knee joints and should touch the floor. Your face should be in between the knee joints. Maintain this pose for five to ten seconds. Now, sit straight and your finger should hold the big toe of your leg.

- Now raise your head and sit straight with your hands beside the ears, just like in Step (b). Slowly bring your body back to the position it was in Step (a). Now breathe normally.

- Repeat this *asana* three or four times.

28. *Physiological factors determining components of physical fitness are*

(*i*) **Muscular Strength** This is the maximum force or tension a muscle or a muscle group can exert against a resistance. Physiologically the muscle will increase in strength only if it has to increase its workload beyond what is ordinarily required of it.

(*ii*) **Power** This is the ability of the body to release maximum muscle contraction in the shortest possible time.

(*iii*) **Speed** This is the rapidity with which one can repeat successive movements of the same pattern.

(*iv*) **Muscular Endurance** This is the ability of a muscle or muscle group to perform repeated contractions against a resistance / load or to sustain contraction for an extended period of time with less discomfort and more rapid recovery.

(*v*) **Agility** This is the ability of a person to change direction or body position as quickly as possible and regain body control to proceed with another movement.

(*vi*) **Flexibility** This is a quality of the muscles, ligaments and tendons that enables the joints of the body to move easily through a complete range of movements.

or

The cardiorespiratory system consists of organs responsible for taking in oxygen for respiration and releasing carbon dioxide and water vapour, which are the waste products formed during respiration. The passages in the nose, windpipe (trachea), bronchi, lungs and air sacs are the main organs of the respiratory system.

A trainer can improve the cardiorespiratory system with the help of exercise by

(i) **Decrease in Rate of Respiration** When a beginner starts exercise, then his rate of respiration increases. But when the same individual performs exercise daily, then his rate of respiration decreases in comparison to the beginning stage at rest.

(ii) **Lung Volume** For normal breathing at rest, lung expand and there is a change in air pressure. During exercise, due to rapid movement of diaphragm and intercostal muscles, total area of lung expands to accommodate more exchange of gases.

(iii) **Lung Diffusion Capacity** During exercise, the lung diffusion capacity increases in both trained and untrained persons.

However, trained athletes may increase their diffusion capacity 30% more than that of an untrained person because athlete's lung surface area and red blood cell count is higher than that of non-athletes.

(iv) **Pulmonary Ventilation** The amount of air passing through lungs each minute is called Pulmonary Ventilation.

The Pulmonary Ventilation (PV) is a producet of Tidal Volume (TV and Respiratory Rate (RR) and therefore at rest it is around 8 l/min.

During exercise time both TV and RR increase, due to which PV will also increase depending on the intensity of exercise.

For an ordinary person, the value of PV may be 40-50 l/min and for well trained athlete, it may be around 100 l/min.

(v) **Residual Air Volume** It is the volume of air in the lungs which is left after exhalation. With exercises, the residual air capacity increases which enhances efficiency of lungs.

29. The Chair Sit and Reach Test is a part of the Senior Fitness Test Protocol, and is designed to test the functional fitness of seniors.

The purpose is to measure lower body flexibility.

The equipments required to perform this test are ruler, a chair with straight back or folding chair (seat 17 inch/ 44 cm high).

Procedure is as follows
- The subject sits on the edge of the chair placed against a wall for safety.
- One foot must remain flat on the floor. The other leg is extended forward with the knee straight, heel touching the floor, with ankle bent at 90°.
- Place one hand on top of the other with tips of the middle fingers even, exhale and reach forward towards the toes by bending at the hip. Keep the back straight and head up.
- Avoid bouncing or quick movements and never stretch to the point of pain. Keep the knee straight and hold the reach for 2 seconds.

The distance to be measured is between the finger tips and the toes. If the finger tips touch the toes, then the score is zero.

If they do not touch, measure the distance between the fingers and the toes (a negative score); if they overlap, measure by how much distance (a positive score). Perform two trials and record the better score.

or

The procedure of measuring height accurately in BMI is given below
- Remove the participant's shoes, bulky clothing, and hair ornaments, and unbraid hair that interferes with the measurement.
- Take the height measurement on flooring that is not carpeted and against a flat surface such as a wall with no molding.
- Have the participant stand with feet flat, together, and back against the wall. Make sure legs are straight, arms are at sides, and shoulders are level.
- Make sure the participant is looking straight ahead and that the line of sight is parallel with the floor.
- Take the measurement while the participant stands with head, shoulders, buttocks, and heels touching the flat surface (wall). Depending on the overall body shape of the participant, all points may not touch the wall.
- Use a flat headpiece to form a right angle with the wall and lower the headpiece until it firmly touches the crown of the head.
- Make sure the measurer's eyes are at the same level as the headpiece.
- Lightly mark where the bottom of the headpiece meets the wall.
- Then, use a metal tape to measure from the base on the floor to the marked measurement on the wall to get the height measurement.
- Accurately record the height to the nearest 0.1 centimeter.

30. Pinki will perform the Harvard step test to measure the cardio vascular fitness of all the trainees. This is because, the test measures the ability of the heart and lungs to supply blood to the muscle tissues. This is essential for performing aerobic activities. The test can be tested on large group and requires very little equipments. It also gives accurate results.

The Harvard Step Test is a test that measures the cardiovascular fitness or aerobic fitness by checking the recovery rate. It was developed by Brouha and his associates in 1943.

The equipments required to perform the test are bench of 20 inches high and stopwatch.

Procedure is as follows :

- The performer steps up and down 30 times a minute on the bench.
- Each time the subject should step all the way up on the bench with the body erect.
- The stepping exercise continues for exactly 5 minutes, unless the performer is forced to stop sooner due to exhaustion.
- As soon as he stops exercising, the performer sists on a quietly while pulse rates are counted at 1 to 1.5, 2 to 2.5 and 3 to 3.5 minutes after the person takes the last formula Fitness index score

$$= \frac{\text{Duration of exercise in seconds} \times 100}{2 \times \text{Sum of pulse counts in recovery}}$$

Sample Paper 2

Physical Education (Unsolved)

(A Highly Simulated Practice Question Paper for CBSE Class XII Examination)

General Instructions

- The question paper consists of 30 questions.
- All questions are compulsory.
- Question 1-12 (Multiple Choice Questions) carry 1 mark each.
- Question 13-16 carrying 2 marks each should be in approximately 30-50 words.
- Question 17-26 carrying 3 marks each should be in approximately 75-100 words.
- Question 27-30 carrying 5 marks each should be in approximately 155-200 words.

Time : 3 hours   **Max. Marks : 80**

1. The Reception Committee for a tournament is responsible for .... (1)
   (a) welcoming the participants
   (b) arranging accommodation and meals for the participants
   (c) proper upkeep of the venues
   (d) welcoming the Chief Guest and spectators at the opening and closing ceremonies

   or Which of the following procedures is not used for drawing up fixtures for a knock-out tournament?
   (a) Staircase   (b) Seeding
   (c) Byes   (d) Special seeding

2. Which of the following is not a type of movement related to physical activity? (1)
   (a) Abduction   (b) Adduction
   (c) Extension   (d) None of these

3. Which of the following is a psychological attribute in sports? (1)
   (a) Self-esteem
   (b) Mental imagery
   (c) Goal setting
   (d) All of the above

   or Jung classified most of the people as ....
   (a) Extroverts   (b) Ambiverts
   (c) Mesomorphs   (d) Introverts

4. Which of the following is a non-nutritive component of diet? (1)
    (a) Fibre   (b) Caffeine
    (c) Water   (d) All of these

5. The corrective measures for Lordosis include ……… (1)
    (a) performing Chakrasana
    (b) performing Paschimottasana
    (c) bending the head backwards while standing
    (d) All of the above

6. Which of the following organisation helps promoting adaptive sports? (1)
    (a) Special Olympics   (b) Deaflympics
    (c) Paralympics   (d) All of these

7. Traits like insight, imagination, receptivity of new ideas are associated with
    (a) Agreeableness
    (b) Extroversion
    (c) Openness
    (d) Neuroticism (1)
or Unintentional physical harm is known as ……. .
    (a) Hostile aggression   (b) Instrumental aggression
    (c) Assertive aggression   (d) Negative aggression

8. Biomechanics is branch of physics in combination with ……… which understands the human movements in a scientific way. (1)
    (a) chemistry   (b) sociology
    (c) biology   (d) psychology

9. Genu Valgum is also known as (1)
    (a) Flat foot   (b) Knock-Knee
    (c) Bow leg   (d) Round shoulders

10. In this condition, the bones become porous, brittle and break easily? (1)
    (a) Amenorrhea   (b) Osteoporosis
    (c) Oligomenorrhea   (d) None of these

11. **Assertion** (A) Everyone should do yoga daily.
    Reason (R) Yoga helps in avoiding various lifestyle disease such as diabetes, obesity and cardiovascular disease. (1)
    Codes
    (a) Both A and R are true and R is the correct explanation of A
    (b) Both A and R are true, but R is not the correct explanation of A
    (c) A is true, but R is false
    (d) A is false, but R is true

12. Match List I with List II.   **(1)**

	List I		List II
A.	50 M Sprint test	1.	Measure Cardiovascular Endurance
B.	600 M Walk test	2.	Abdominal Strength
C.	Sit and Reach test	3.	Determine Speed
D.	Partial Curl-up test	4.	Flexibility of Low Back

Codes

(a) A-1, B-2, C-3, D-4   (b) A-2, B-4, C-3, D-1

(c) A-3, B-1, C-4, D-2   (d) A-4, B-3, C-2, D-1

13. Identity the asana show below.   **(2)**

(a)    (b)

(c)    (d)

14. Identify the injury and give their names.   **(2)**

(a) 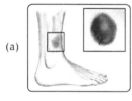   (b)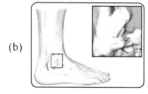

(c) 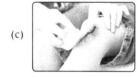   (d)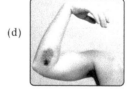

15. Design a freehand four exercises programme for lordosis.   **(2)**

16. Differentiate between basic endurance and speed endurance.   (2)

or

What are the salient features of the Fartlek training method?

17. Below given is the BMI data of a student of primary school's check-up.

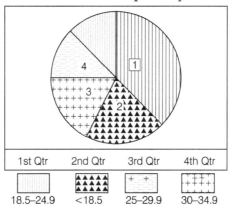

On the basis of the above data; answer the following questions:

(i) In which category does the major students population falls into?   (1)
  (a) Obese   (b) Normal weight
  (c) Under weight   (d) Over weight

(ii) The school has to develop an activity based program to decrease the number of   (1)

  (a)   (b) [image]   (c) [image]   (d) [image]

(iii) Which category is related to obese?   (1)

  (a) [image]   (b) [image]   (c) [image]   (d) [image]

18. Anuj is a student of class XIIth and is suffering from flatfoot. During a recent medical check-up at school, he was advised to practice yoga and participate in sports activities for curing it.

Based on this case answer the following questions.

(i) The yoga instructor of the school has asked to perform   (1)
  (a) walk on inner edge of foot   (b) run on inner edge of foot
  (c) shavasana   (d) trikonasana

(ii) Due to flatfoot, a person faces lot of problems while   (1)
  (a) sleeping and sitting   (b) standing and walking
  (c) sitting and walking   (d) sleeping and walking

(iii) The common remedies for flatfoot is/are   (1)
  (a) skip on rope   (b) walking on toes
  (c) stand up and down on the heels   (d) All of these

19. Compare the first and second law of Newton with their application in sports. (3)

or "Friction is a necessary evil." Justify your answer with suitable example from sport.

20. Create a flow chart for dimensions, types and traits of personality. (3)

21. Explain the procedure of giving Bye in fixture. (3)

or Discuss about pre-meet responsibilities of sports committees.

22. Enlist all the postural deformities of the spine. Explain any two of these deformities. (3)

23. Explain the importance of vitamin C and its various sources. (3)

24. What is importance of Paralympics? (3)

25. Which test is carried out to measure the upper body flexibility of senior citizens? Explain it. (3)

26. Explain the computing BHR. (3)

or Briefly explain amenorrhea. How it is associated with women athletes.

27. What do you mean by sports committee? Explain any three. (5)

28. Which yogic asanas are helpful in relieving hypertension? Describe the procedure for performing two such asana. (5)

or Briefly explain the administration of Pawanmuktasana along with its contraindications and draw stick diagram.

29. Suggest the formation of various committees for systematic and smooth conduct of sports day in your school. (5)

or Following the suggested guidelines, draw a fixture of 12 teams in a league-cum knock-out tournament.

30. Gym trainer Radhika conducts the Cardiovascular fitness test of all her trainees once a month. Explain exercise on cardio Respiratory System. (5)

Answers

1. (d) welcoming the Chief Guest and spectators at the opening and closing ceremonies

   or   (a) Staircase

2. (d) None of these

3. (d) All of these   or (b) Ambiverts

4. All of these

5. (a) performing Chakrasana

6. (d) All of these

7. (c) Openess

   or (b) Instrumental aggression

8. (c) biology

9. (b) Knock-knee

10. (b) Osteoporosis

11. (a) Both A and R are true and R is the correct explanation of A.

12. (c) 3 1 4 2

13. (a) Gomukhasana   (b) Pavanamuktasana   (c) Urdhva Hastasana   (d) Halasana (Plow Poss)

14. (a) Contusion   (d) Abrasion   (b) Sprain   (c) Laceration

Sample Paper 3

Physical Education (Unsolved)

(A Highly Simulated Practice Question Paper for CBSE Class XII Examination)

General Instructions

- The question paper consists of 30 questions.
- All questions are compulsory.
- Question 1-12 (Multiple Choice Questions) carry 1 mark each.
- Question 13-16 carrying 2 marks each should be in approximately 30-50 words.
- Question 17-26 carrying 3 marks each should be in approximately 75-100 words.
- Question 27-30 carrying 5 marks each should be in approximately 155-200 words.

Time : 3 hours **Max. Marks : 80**

1. Which of the following is a contraindication for Shavasana? (1)
   - (a) Liver enlargement
   - (b) Obesity
   - (c) High blood pressure
   - (d) None of these

   or Asthma can be reduced by performing .... and ....
   - (a) Sukhasana, Trikonasana
   - (b) Chakrasana, Tadasana
   - (c) Ardh Matsyendrasana, Matsyasana
   - (d) None of these

2. Out of the following methods which one is not used for development of flexibility? (1)
   - (a) Pace run method
   - (b) Slow stretching
   - (c) Post-Isometric stretching
   - (d) Ballistic

3. It is the fracture which occurs when a bone bends and cracks, instead of breaking completely into separate pieces. (1)
   - (a) Transverse
   - (b) Comminuted
   - (c) Green Stick
   - (d) Impacted

   or Fractures may be classified as .... and ....
   - (a) severe, moderate
   - (b) open, closed
   - (c) broken, hairline
   - (d) None of these

4. Which of the following is an important test for children with age group 5-8 years?
   (a) Plate Tapping   (b) Flamingo Balance
   (c) 600 m run/walk   (d) Both (a) and (b)

5. A push up is which form of exercise?   (1)
   (a) Aerobic   (b) Isometric
   (c) Isokinetic   (d) Isotonic

6. Which of the following procedures is not used for drawing up fixtures for a knockout
   tournament?   (1)
   (a) Bye   (b) Seeding
   (c) Staircase   (d) Special seeding

7. In which year the International Paralympic Committee was founded?   (1)
   (a) 22nd September, 1989   (b) 22nd September, 1990
   (c) 20th September, 1989   (d) 20th September, 1992

or Where was the first Special Olympic games held in 1968?
   (a) Shanghai   (b) Los Angeles
   (c) Chicago   (d) New Haven

8. Which of the following is the shortest training cycle?   (1)
   (a) Meso Cycle   (b) Macro Cycle
   (c) Micro Cycle   (d) None of these

9. The duration of Arm Curl Test is   (1)
   (a) 30 seconds   (b) 15 seconds
   (c) 20 seconds   (d) 25 seconds

10. .... is a combination of speed and endurance abilities.   (1)
   (a) Speed Endurance   (b) Locomotor Ability
   (c) Movement Speed   (d) Reaction Speed

11. Given below are the two statements labelled as Assertion (A) and
   Reason (R).   (1)
   Assertion (A) The incidence of menstrual dysfunction in women has increased.
   Reason (R) There has been increased in participation of women in physical fitness
   and competitive endurance sports.
   Codes
   (a) Both A and R are true and R is the correct explanation of A
   (b) Both A and R are true, but R is not the correct explanation of A
   (c) A is true, but R is false
   (d) A is false, but R is true

12. Match List I with List II. (1)

	List I		List II
A	Iron	1.	Nervous system
B	Sodium	2.	Haemoglobin
C	Fluorine	3.	Strong bone
D	Phosphorus	4.	Enamel

Codes

(a) A-3, B-4, C-2, D-1   (b) A-4, B-1, C-3, D-2

(c) A-1, B-3, C-2, D-4   (d) A-2, B-1, C-4, D-3

13. Identity the types of asanas. (2)

(a)

(b)

(c)

(d)

14. Identify the bone fracture and give their name (2)

(a)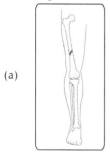
(b)
(c)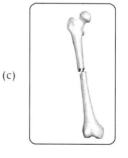
(d)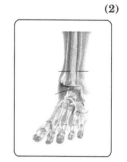

15. Design a free hand four exercises programme for curring asthma. (2)

16. Differentiate between nutritive and non nutritive components of diet giving two points of each. (2)

or Differentiate between the composition of carbohydrates and fats.

17. Below given is the BMI data of a student of Art stream of class 12th health check-up.

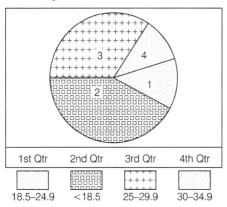

On the basis of the above data; answer the following questions.

(i) In which category does the least students' population falls into? (1)
  (a) Normal weight   (b) Under weight
  (c) Obese   (d) Over weight

(ii) The school has to develop an activity based program to increase the number of (1)

  (a) ▦   (b) ▭   (c) ▨   (d) ⊞

(iii) Which category is related to over weight? (1)

  (a) ▭   (b) ▦   (c) ⊞   (d) ▨

18. Neha is a student of class VI and is suffering from kyphosis. During a recent medical check-up at school she was adviced to practice yoga and participate in sports activities for curing it.

Based on this case answer the following questions.

(i) The yoga instructor of the school has asked to perform. (1)
  (a) Tadasana   (b) Pawanamukhasana
  (c) Matsyasana   (d) Dhanurasana

(ii) Due to kyphosis,Neha would develop which postural deformities. (1)
  (a) depression of chest   (b) bowteg
  (c) knock-knee   (d) flatfoot

(iii) Which of the following is/are not cause of kyphosis? (1)
  (a) Malnutrition   (b) Carrying heavy loads on waist
  (c) Weak muscles   (d) Shyness among girls

19. Discuss in detail about Paralympic Games. (3)

or Explain the advantages of physical activities for children with special needs.

20. Create a flow chart for the types of test and measurement in sports. (3)

21. What is the difference between Discipline committee and Reception committee? (3)

or Make a knock-out fixture for 7 teams.

22. What are the uses of any three minerals in our diet? (3)

23. Enlist the Benefits of Vakrasana. (3)

24. What do you understand by Paralympics? Explain in brief. (3)

25. Explain the advantages of Fartlek training. (3)

26. Explain the staircase method of a league tournament for 7 teams. (3)

or Explain how dislocation of a bone joint is managed.

27. What is friction? Is it advantageous or disadvantageous in the field of games and sports? (5)

28. Explain the contraindications of Halasana, Ardha Matsyendrasana and Urdhva Hastasana. (5)

or Explain various asanas : Shavasana, Bhujangasana, Shalabhasana, Mandukasana and Vakrasana.

29. Explain the structure of personality. Describe the role of sports in developing the personality. (5)

or Write any three personality types that are formulated by Carl Jung.

30. Gymnast trainer John, asks his students to pad their palms with lime powder always before practising in horizontal bars. Why he says so? What will happen if students don't use lime powder before practicing. (5)

Answers

1. (*d*) None of these   *or*   (*c*) Chakrasana, Tadasana
2. (*a*) Pace run method
3. (*c*) Green stick   *or*   (*b*) open, closed
4. (*d*) Both (a) and (b)
5. (*b*) Isometric
6. (*c*) Staircase
7. (*a*) 22nd September, 1989   *or*   (*c*) Chicago
8. (*c*) Micro Cycle
9. (*a*) 30 seconds
10. (*a*) Speed Endurance
11. (*a*) Both A and R are true and R is the correct explanation of A
12. (*d*) 2 1 4 3
13. (a) Vakrasana   (b) Ardha Matsyendrasana   (c) Katichakrasana   (d) Shalabhasana
14. (a) Comminuted Fracture   (b) Greenstick Fracture   (c) Transverse Fracture
    (d) Ankle Dislocation

CPSIA information can be obtained
at www.ICGtesting.com
Printed in the USA
LVHW051620181122
733280LV00007B/566